Australia in Oxfor

CW00919595

Made possible by a generous grant from

The News Corporation Ltd
and
News International p.l.c.

Captain Charles Sturt's expedition of 1830 on the Murray River. Watercolour and sketches by Charles Sturt. The watercolour and sketches were discovered during conservation work at the Bodleian Library for the exhibition *Australia in Oxford: The Visual Image*. They were revealed on the back of one of Sturt's sketch maps of the Murray River when an old backing sheet, which had been pasted over it, was removed. (Rhodes House Library Ms.Austral.s.4.fol.34verso)

Australia in Oxford

edited by

Howard Morphy and Elizabeth Edwards

Pitt Rivers Museum
University of Oxford
Monograph 4

made possible by a generous grant from

The News Corporation Ltd. and News International p.l.c.

ISBN: 0 902793 225
ISSN: 0141-2477

Printed in England by
Stephen Austin and Sons Ltd. Hertford

Cover illustrations:

Front cover: section of a Queensland rainforest
shield, Hardy Collection, Pitt Rivers Museum
1900.55.165.

Back cover: "First interview of the English with the
women of Port Jackson in New South Wales."
Late 18th century watercolour by R. Willet Miller
after Lieut. William Bradley.
(Ashmolean Museum, Hope Collection)

Contents

Australia in Oxford Exhibition

Acknowledgements

We are most grateful to the following institutions who have given us access to and use of their material: Ashmolean Museum (Department of Western Art), Curators of the Bodleian Library, Trustees of the British Museum (Natural History), Exeter College, Lincoln College, Museum of the History of Science, Department of Plant Sciences, Radcliffe Science Library, Rhodes House Library, Department of Zoology, and finally the University of Sydney and the Western Australian Museum.

We should also like to thank the following for all their advice and assistance: Brian Atkins, Alan Bell, Emma Chambers, Jim Hull, Tom Kemp, Jim Kennedy, Gillian King, Ken McNamara, Frances Morphy, Monica Price, Susie Rayner, Nicholas Penny, Nicolas Peterson, Fiona Piddock, Phil Powell, Tony Simcock, Barbara Spencer, Peter Sutton, John Whiteley and Dr. F. White.

Foreword

From the perspective of its Aboriginal inhabitants, Europe and Europeans had no existence for the first fifty thousand years of human history in Australia. For much of its recent history since the arrival in 1788 of the First Fleet the relationship with Europe has been crucial in defining the identity of Australia and Australians. The Aborigines symbolise autonomy from Europe, the First Fleet the beginning of encapsulation. The tension between the two has been a major theme of the last two hundred years of Australian history.

European perceptions of Australia had been partly formed in the European imagination long before the reality of the continent was known. It was a hypothetical land in the South, rich in promise, and it simply had to exist. And when it was 'discovered' and opened up by Europeans, and the pieces of the jigsaw were fitted together, it was at first much misunderstood. Seen through European eyes little was there that had been anticipated and hoped for, no vast inland seas, no great freshwater lakes, apparently no great riches and resources. Many of the things which motivated the exploration of Australia turned out to be illusions and so much that was there remained invisible. Much of Australia was unfamiliar, yet at the start it had to be seen through European eyes, which often either romanticised what was seen or distorted it. The Australian landscape, its plants and animals and the Aborigines who occupied it were all viewed unsympathetically, through prejudiced and blinkered eyes. The early chapters in this book explore some of the early understandings of Australia and the images of Australia which accumulated in Oxford's collections and tell how in some cases new understandings have emerged as Australia in turn has fought back to impose itself on the European imagination.

Oxford as one of the great archives of knowledge has some important collections from Australia's recent past. Among them are Dampier's album pages of pressed flowers collected a hundred years before the First Fleet, Sturt's papers of his explorations of the Murray River and Central Australia and the papers of the pioneer biologist and anthropologist Sir Baldwin Spencer. If in individual cases the items arrived as a result of chance, sentiment or loyalty, the whole reflects the dual role Oxford played in exploring the world intellectually and, particularly in the 19th century, in trying to influence its shape. The later chapters of this book look at the influence of Oxford in the development of 19th century universities in Australia and finally at the emergence of an Australia which exists independent of the European imagination and which is positioning itself independently in the academic as well as in the political world.

Zelman Cowen

Figure 2. *Clianthus formosus* 'Sturt's desert pea'. Specimen collected by William Dampier in 1699 and now in the Sherardian Herbarium in Oxford.

1. William Dampier and his Botanical Collections

by Serena K. Marner

A small but unique collection of dried plants collected in 1699 by the circumnavigator and buccaneer William Dampier is today preserved in the Sherardian Herbarium of the Department of Plant Sciences at the University of Oxford. This collection is significant in two respects: it is the earliest documented collection of Australian flora and Dampier himself was the first Englishman to make any record of a visit to Australia. Dampier landed on the shores of Western Australia some 71 years before the more renowned landing of Sir Joseph Banks and Captain Cook in Botany Bay.

Dampier was born at East Coker near Yeovil in Somerset in 1652. In 1688 he visited what was then New Holland for the first time in a ship called the "Cygnet". After leaving the shores of Australia Dampier had an arguement with the ships Captain and left the ship at Nicobar. He found his way to Sumatra and finally returned to England in 1691. The Earl of Pembroke brought him to the attention of King William III who

placed him in command of H.M.S. Roebuck. He then set off on a voyage of discovery which took him to Bahia in Brazil before going on to Australia. It was on this occasion that he made his collection of plants. He continued his journey sailing on to Timor and along the north coast of New Guinea. On his return journey misfortune struck when the ship sprung a leak off Ascension Island and had to be abandoned. Miraculously the botanical specimens were salvaged and safeguarded through a hazardous period while he and his crew 'lived on goats and turtle'. Eventually Dampier was rescued by the "Canterbury", an East-India ship, that called at the Island and he returned home with little else than the clothes he wore, his journal and his herbarium.

When Dampier visited Australia it was still a largely unknown land, 'Terra Australis Incognita'. On the 5th January 1688 Dampier wrote of the country "New Holland is a very large Tract of Land. It is not yet determined whether it is an Island or a Continent, but I am

Figure 3. Portrait of William Dampier engraved by Sherwin.
Hope Collection. Ashmolean Museum.

1

certain that it joins neither to Asia, Africa, nor America.". Eleven years later in August 1699 he went ashore at what he called Sharks Bay, principally to find fresh water. As an explorer in an unknown land, perhaps not surprisingly, Dampier collected plants that were either unusual or unfamiliar to him or plants that he recognised as similar to those he already knew.

One of the most interesting plants that Dampier collected was *Clianthus formosus* (G. Don.) Ford & Vickery, 'Sturt's desert pea'. He was the first European to find this plant with strikingly attractive flowers. The whole plant has a creeping habit and the flowers are bright red, each having a bulbous black 'eye'. A plant that interested Dampier for quite different reasons was 'Dampier's Rosemary'. He wrote of it in his journal "There grow here 2 or 3 sorts of Shrubs, one just like Rosemary; and therefore I called this 'Rosemary' Island. It grew in plenty here, but had no smell.". The specimen he collected was subsequently described as *Eurybia dampieri* (A. Cunn.) ex DC.

Some of the other plants collected by Dampier were later found to be of previously unknown genera. When Robert Brown, who was to become the first Keeper of Botany at the British Museum, examined the collection in the early nineteenth century, he commemorated Dampier by naming a genus after him – *Dampiera* in the family Goodeniaceae. Dampiers' specimen labelled as "Leucoium maritimum Nov. Hollandicum, fol. parva, incano, fl. amplo, caeruleo" was therefore named *Dampiera incana* R. Br. Another genus unknown before Dampier collected it was *Hannafordia* in the family Sterculiaceae. His specimen has been named as *Hannafordia quadrivalis* F. Muell.

When Dampier returned to England he passed his plant specimens on to 'the ingenious Dr. Woodward'. Woodward was a friend of William Sherard, who founded the Sherardian Chair of Botany in Oxford, and in 1710 handed over to him his entire collection of plants including the Dampier material. Some of the specimens had previously been sent to John Ray 'the Father of English Natural History' who was completing his great botanical work entitled 'Historia Plantarum'. Descriptions of several Dampier specimens appear as an appendix to the third volume published in 1704, and the plants of New Holland thus began to enter the botanical literature. However they are not mentioned as much as might have been expected in later publications as the collection was not made available to George Bentham or Ferdinand von Mueller when writing "Flora Australiensis" (1863 – 1878).

In the preface of his book 'A Voyage to New Holland etc. in the year 1699', Dampier writes that he hopes the Third Volume of his Voyages would be acceptable to those readers who are curious to know the nature of the inhabitants, animals, plants, soil, etc. of distant countries which have not been visited by any Europeans before. He writes "It has almost always been the Fate of those who have made new Discoveries, to be disesteemed and lightly spoken of . . ." "But this Satisfaction I am sure of having, that the Things themselves in the Discovery of which I have been imployed, are most worthy of our Dilligentest Search and Inquiry; being the various and wonderful Works of God in different Parts of the World : And however unfit a Person I may be in other respects to have undertaken this Task, yet at least I have given a faithful Account, and have found some Things undiscovered by any before, and which may at least be some Assistance and Direction to better qualified Persons who shall come after me."

REFERENCES

Dampier, William, 1703 'A Voyage to New Holland etc. in the Year 1699.' Vol. III of 'A New Voyage Round the World.' 1703. London: James Knapton.

Lee, Ida, 1905, Early Explorers in Australia. 1925. London: Methuen.

Osborn, T. G. B. and C. A. Gardner. 1938, Dampier's Australian Plants. *Proceedings of the Linnean Society of London*: 44–50.

Shipman, J. C. 1962. William Dampier.

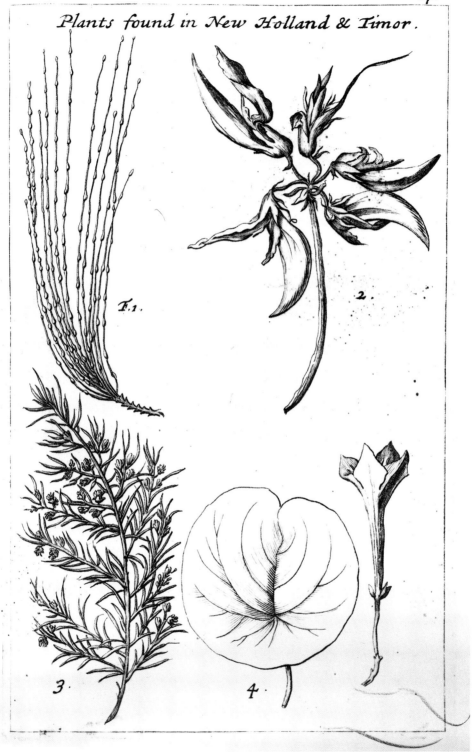

Figure 4. Page of Volume III of Dampier's *A new voyage around the world*.

Alcyone azurea.

2. The Peculiar Natural History of New Holland

by Steve Simpson

The Victorian era was the golden age for the study of Natural History. As collectors brought more and more specimens, both dead and alive, back to England from the Colonies and other far-flung places, it became clear that institutions were required, not only for the storage and display of such material, but also for research and teaching. Dr. Henry Acland, who was then Reader in Anatomy, pressed for such a facility in the University of Oxford. He managed, despite considerable opposition from many members of the University, to get a resolution passed for the building of a museum in Oxford to house "all the materials explanatory of the structure of the earth, and of the organic beings placed upon it". The result was the University Museum, an Italian Gothic structure completed in 1860, which became home to the Departments of Astronomy, Geometry, Experimental Physics, Mineralogy, Chemistry, Geology, Zoology, Anatomy, Physiology, and Medicine. Over the following years the Departments vacated the University Museum for new premises as their requirements outgrew the building. The first to go was Physics, in 1872, and the last, the Hope Department of Zoology (Entomology), in 1978. Now the Museum exists primarily to preserve, curate and research the University's extensive and important zoological, entomological, geological and mineralogical collections. Amongst these collections are numerous specimens from Australia, many of which were donated by early collectors and naturalists. The strangeness of such specimens posed some of the most intriguing riddles facing the Victorian students of Natural History.

The natural history of Australia is peculiar. That much is common knowledge. Even the first mariners from Europe, who must surely have been inured to the bizarre during their travels, were impressed, even distressed, by the oddness of Australia's fauna and flora. Consider, for example, William Dampier's response to a lizard encountered in 1699:

". . . a sort of Guano's, of the same shape and size with other Guano's describ'd . . . but differing from them in three Particulars: For these had a larger and uglier Head; and had no Tail: And at the rump, instead of a Tail there, they had a stump of a Tail, which appear'd like another Head; but not really such, being without Mouth or Eyes: Yet this Creature seem'd by this means to have a Head at each end; and, which may be reckon'd a fourth difference, the Legs also seem'd all four of them to be Fore-legs, being all alike in shape and length, and seeming by the Joints and Bending to be made as if they were to go indifferently either Head or Tail foremost. They were speckled black and yellow like Toads, and had Scales or Knobs like those of Crocodiles, plated on to the Skin, or stuck into it, as part of the Skin. They are very slow in motion; and when a Man comes nigh them they stand still and hiss, not endeavouring to get away. Their livers are also spotted black and yellow: and the Body when opened hath a very unsavoury Smell. I did not see such ugly Creatures any where but here. The Guano's I have observed to be very good Meat: and I have often eaten of Snakes, Croco-

Figure 5. One of the most renowned ornithologists of the Victorian era was John Gould, a London taxidermist. In 1838 he travelled to Australia and was astonished by the 'curious habits' and novelty of the birds. It was Gould who was responsible for introducing the budgerigar to pet shops in Britain. The *Birds of Australia,* which included 600 superb colour plates, was published in 1840-48 and remains a classic work. The illustration shown here (Azure kingfishers, *Alcyone azurea*) is unique, being a copy of a Gould plate taken from a folio entitled *Selections from Gould's Birds of Australia,* by Eliza and Louisa Westcombe. The volume resides in the Alexander Library, Department of Zoology, Oxford, and was 'Presented by Mary E. Pumphrey Oct. 1953 about a century after the paintings were made by her great aunts E. & L. Westcombe'.

diles and Allegators, and many Creatures that look frightfully enough, and there are but few I should have been afraid to eat of if prest by Hunger, yet I think my Stomach would scarce have serv'd to venture upon these *N. Holland* Guano's, both the Looks and the Smell of them being so offensive." (Dampier, 1703)

Dampier was not overly enthusiastic about what he saw of Australia's west coast. As well as the hideousness of its lizards, its lack of fresh water and generally inhospitable appearance, he noted that the seas were full of sharks.

"The Sea-fish that we saw here (for here was no River, Land or Pond of Fresh Water to be seen) are chiefly Sharks. There are abundance of them in this particular Sound, that I therefore gave it the Name of Shark's Bay." (*ibid.*)

Every cloud has its silver lining, however, and

Dampier's stomach did serve to venture upon the only mammal discovered in forays ashore.

". . . a sort of Raccoons, different from those of the West Indies, chiefly as to their Legs; for these have very short fore Legs; but go jumping upon them as the others do, and like them are very good Meat . . ." (*ibid.*)

This was probably a Banded Hare Wallaby, later described by C.A. Lesueur from specimens taken in 1801. Other early descriptions of kangaroos and wallabies are intriguing. The first recorded description is that of Pelsart who was aboard the ill-fated ship "Batavia" which was wrecked on the coast of Western Australia in 1629. Sir Joseph Banks, one of the two biologists (Sir Daniel Solander was the other) aboard Captain James Cook's *Endeavour* in 1770 apparently had not read Pelsart's account (although, to be

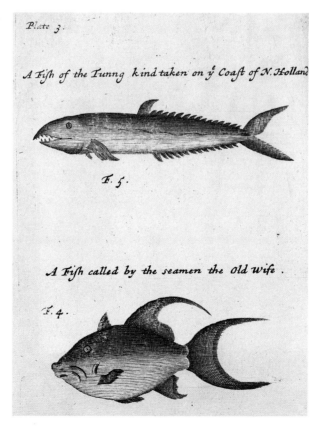

Figures 6 and 7. Two plates from Dampier's (1703) account of his voyage to New Holland, illustrating (not altogether accurately) various fish and sea birds encountered.

Place this P. 123.

F. 3.

A Noddy of N. Holland. P.123 & 143.

F. 5.

The head & greatest part of y neck of this bird is red, & therein differs from the Avosetta of Italy.

A Comon Noddy. P. 143

F. 6.

F. 4.

The Bill & Leggs of this Bird are of a Bright Red.

fair, Pelsart did call them cats) and wrote of his first experiences of the unusual creatures in a series of entries in his journal.

22nd June 1770 at Endeavour River, where the ship was being repaired following its hitting a coral bombora on June 10th:

"Myself employed all day in laying in plants; the people who were sent to the other side of the water to shoot pigeons, saw an animal as large as a greyhound, of a mouse colour, and very swift . . ."

25th June:

"In gathering plants today I had the good fortune to see the beast so much talked of, though but imperfectly; he was not only like a grey-hound in size and running, but had a tail as long as any greyhound's; what to liken him to I could not tell, nothing that I have seen at all resembles him."

It should be said that Banks's preoccupation with greyhounds comes from his actually having one on board ship as a pet, as is mentioned in the entry of 7th July:

"We walked many miles over the flats and saw four of the animals, two of which my greyhound fairly chased; but they beat him owing to the length and thickness of the grass, which preven-ted him from running, while they at every bound leapt over the tops of it. We observed, much to our surprise, that instead of going upon all fours, this animal went only upon two legs, making vast bounds just like a jerboa (*Mus jaculus*) does."

Banks was later to call the creature *kangaroo*, the name given to one species in the Guugu

Yimidhirr language, spoken by the local Aboriginal group (Haviland, 1979).

Governor Arthur Phillip commented further on the kangaroo and its relationship with the jerboa in his account of the establishment of the first colony in Sydney Cove, published in 1789.

"The kangaroo, though it resembles the jerboa in the peculiarity of using only the hinder legs in progression, does not belong to that genus. The pouch of the female, in which the young are nursed, is thought to connect it rather with the opossum tribe. This extraordinary formation, hitherto esteemed peculiar to that one [South American] genus, seems, however, in New Holland not to be sufficiently characteristic: it has been found both in the rat and the squirrel kind."

Phillip had, of course, noted the preponderance of marsupials in Australia; mammals which, unlike the more usual placental types, give birth to embryonic young which they suckle to a more reasonable state of development within an external pouch.

Stranger animals were still to be found. A creature which had a pouch and hopped was one thing, one which was furred and warm blooded, yet had a beak like a duck, a tail like a beaver and laid eggs was something else entirely. During the first century of colonization the extraordinary nature of the Australian fauna and flora became abundantly clear as explorers and biologists

THE KANGOOROO.

Published as the Act directs June 15 1789, by J. Stockdale.

Figures 8 and 9. Early, rather exaggerated representations of the kangaroo and spotted opossum, both from Governor Arthur Phillips's (1789) journal

Figure 9.

traversed the continent. The platypus turned out not to be the figment of a beer-crazed imagination. There really were birds that buried their huge eggs in mounds of leaf litter six feet high and twenty feet across and regulated the temperature precisely by adjusting the thickness of the overlying mulch, until the hatchlings emerged, not naked and helpless, but fully fledged and able to fend for themselves from the outset. But why does Australia have such a peculiar array of animals and plants? Why are there so many species of marsupial (two-thirds of the world's fauna, the rest being in South America)? Why is there only one native member of the order Carnivora, and even that is a recent arrival (the dingo)? Why are there no vultures, woodpeckers, bulbuls or barbels, yet numerous species of ducks, crows, kingfishers, pigeons and parrots? Why are the primitive egg-laying mammals, the monotremes, found only in and around Australia? Why is the dominant group of trees, the eucalypts, not found anywhere else in the world, despite the fact that recent years have seen it flourish across much of the globe when introduced as a timber crop?

The foundation for answering questions like this was being established at precisely the same time as the University Museum in Oxford was

J. G. Keulemans, del.

Witherby & C°

CATHETURUS LATHAMI.
(BRUSH -TURKEY)

J. G. Keulemans, del.

Witherby & C°

DROMÆUS DIEMENENSIS.
(TASMANIAN EMU).

Figures 10 and 11. Plates of the brush turkey (now named *Alectura lathami*) and Tasmanian emu (actually an extinct subspecies of the mainland emu, *Dromais novaehollandiae*) from the monumental series *The Birds of Australia* by Gregory M. Mathews, published in twelve volumes and six supplements between 1910 and 1928 (Witherby & Co., London). The brush turkey is a representative of the peculiar family, the Megapodiidae, which incubate their eggs in large mounds of soil and leaf litter (see text). That the emu is a relict of the fauna of Gondwanaland prior to the time when Africa and South America drifted away, is evidenced by the presence of its relatives the ostrich and the rhea in these other continents.

being built, for its construction coincided with the publication of Darwin's "On the Origin of Species by Means of Natural Selection". Indeed, on the 30th of June 1860, during its inaugural year, the Museum was host to one of the most famous debates in biology, between those opposed to Darwin's theory, led by Bishop Wilberforce, and those in support, whose spokesman was Professor Thomas Huxley ("I would rather be descended from an ape than from a divine who employs authority to stifle truth"). While Darwin's theory provided a framework for explaining the diversity and peculiarity of the Australian fauna and flora, a more complete answer to questions such as those posed above did not emerge until the new century, when in 1912 Wegener proposed his theory of drifting continents.

Australia has not always been where it is today. In fact Australia is no longer in precisely the same place it was when Dampier arrived. The spot where he gazed in horror at the Guano's was probably about 10 metres south of its present position. The continent has been moving slowly northward, floating on the fluid mantle of the earth, driven by convection currents; alone for the past 55 million years (or so).

Australia wasn't always alone. It once cohabited with what are now Africa, Madagascar, South America, India, New Zealand and Antarctica in a massive southern super continent called Gondwanaland. Before that it was part of an even larger mass, Pangaea, which in-corporated all the land on earth. Africa was the first to leave Gondwanaland. About 160 million years ago it broke away and travelled north eventually to join Europe. Thirty-five million years later India also broke its moorings, headed north and ploughed into Asia; the collision produced the Himalayas. Eighty million years ago New Zealand split and drifted eastward. Up until 55 million years ago Australia, Antarctica and South America remained together. Since that time they have gone their separate ways. For 40 million years Australia floated alone, carrying a cargo of plants and animals, the legacy of Gond-

wanaland in its various forms. But as the continent moved north it eventually impinged upon the Indonesian archipelago, allowing a succession of new arrivals to board.

Whereas the placental mammals rose to ascendancy in all other continents, driving the marsupials to extinction except in South America, they did not arrive in Australia until bats, rodents, the dingo and humans crossed from Indonesia. The marsupials, left alone for so long, radiated and diversified to occupy the available niches, often becoming highly specialised in the process. The same occurred for plants as well as birds, reptiles, insects and other animals, so that today's flora and fauna have components from the original cargo and other more recent arrivals from the north.

At the time when Gondwanaland finally disintegrated, Australia was probably flat with extensive inland seas and lakes of freshwater. The first European explorers were correct in their predictions of such extensive inland waterways, they were just 50 million years too late. The climate was humid and warm. Since then there have been considerable changes in climate and topography. The lakes dried up and the centre became arid, the Great Dividing Range and the Flinders and Mount Lofty Ranges were formed, the Ice Ages came and went. Australia as we now know it was formed.

The processes of change in landscape and natural history have accelerated dramatically during the past 200 hundred years of European colonization. Apart from the obvious effects of increased urbanization, industry, mining and farming, there has been a surge in the number of foreign plant and animal species arriving. The domestic cat, the rabbit, and the prickly pear all demonstrate the problems such immigrants can cause in an environment which has developed for so long in isolation.

Dampier, Captain William 1703. A Voyage to New Holland &c. In the Year, 1699. Vol. III. London, James Knapton, at the Crown in St. Paul's Church Yard.

Haviland, John 1979. Guugu Yimidhirr. In R.M.W. Dixon and B.J. Blake (editors) Handbook of Australian Languages, Vol. 1. Canberra, Australian National University Press.

Hooker, Sir Joseph D. (editor) 1896. Journal of the Right Hon. Sir Joseph Banks during Captain Cook's First Voyage in H.M.S. Endeavour in 1768–71 to Terra del Fuego, Otahite, New Zealand, Australia, the Dutch East Indies, etc. New York, Macmillan.

Phillip, Governor Arthur 1789. The Voyage of Governor Phillip to Botany Bay with an Account of the Establishment of the Colonies of Port Jackson & Norfolk Island. London, John Stockdale.

Australia in the University Museum

Figure 12. Fossilized lower jaw of *Diprotodon,* the largest known marsupial, adults of which were up to 3.5m (11 feet) long. It was allied to the wombats but looked rather like a hairy hippo. From the Pleistocene of the Darling Downs, Queensland.

Figure 13. Fossil shells of the brachiopod *Sulciplica transversa* Waterhouse, from the marine Permian of Eagle Hawk Neck, Tasmania.

Figure 14. *Glossopteris,* the dominant land plant of the flora that covered Gondwanaland in Upper Palaeozoic times (about 250 million years ago). From the Permian deposits of Newcastle, New South Wales.

Figure 15. Precious opal is the most famous of the many gemstones found in Australia.

Figure 16. Australia's economy relies heavily on its rich deposits of ore minerals, including those of copper, here seen in its pure native form.

Figure 17. The Broken Hill mines of New South Wales are renowned for their enormous variety of rare or beautiful minerals, including cerussite (lead carbonate).

Figure 18 opposite.
Two spectacular tropical
butterflies from northern
Australia, the Mountain Blue,
Papilio ulysses, and the Cairns
Birdwing,
Ornithoptera p. euphorion.

Figure 19.
A selection of Australian
beetles, including
representatives from the
families Curculionidae,
Buprestidae, Scarabaeidae
and Lucanidae.

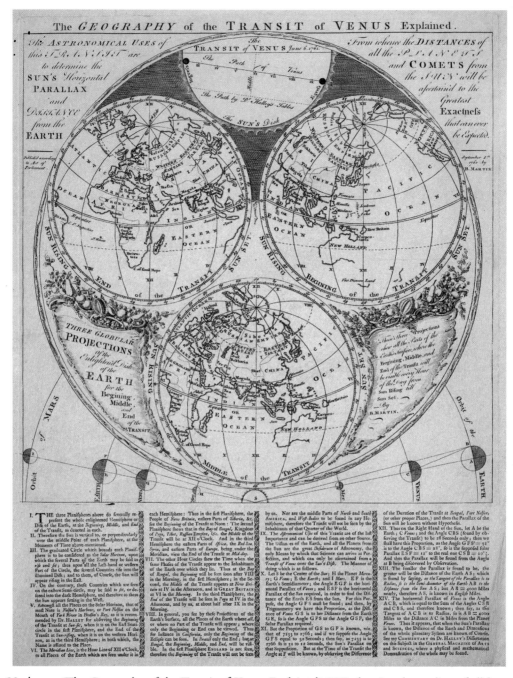

Figure 20 above. 'The Geography of the Transit of Venus Explained' 1760 showing the outline of all but eastern Australia. By B. Martin, a well-known popularizer of science in the mid 18th century. (Museum of the History of Science)

Figure 21 opposite. Detail of a map of the world published in the 1676 edition of John Speed's 'Theatre of Empire'. The amorphous shape of the southern continent is typical of popular representations in the 17th century. (Lincoln College)

3. The Emerging Shape

Although Australia has been inhabited for some 50,000 years (according to current archaeological thinking), European awareness of its existence is less than 500 years old. It is possible that the Portuguese sighted Australia in the early 16th century although the evidence is uncertain. However with the acceptance of the notion that the world is round, the existence of a southern continent became a strong belief on rational if not empirical grounds. The idea of Terra Australis – Terra Incognita, appealed strongly to the European imagination: it was the repository of untold riches, fabulous beasts, of King Solomon's Mines and so on. The increasingly accurate knowledge of the north and west coasts of "New Holland" gathered by Dutch sea-captains during the 17th century and the apparent barrenness of the coastal regions did little to undermine this romantic idea. Indeed at one stage it was believed

that there were two great southern continents. It was only in the second half of the 18th century that the modern European map of Australia emerged. The coastline was largely delineated during Captain Cook's 1st Voyage in 1770. Only the Bass Strait between Australia and Tasmania remained uncharted but this work was completed by the English seamen Flinders and Bass in 1798. Although it was many years until the interior was mapped, the outer shape of Australia had essentially emerged by the turn of the 18th century.

REFERENCES

Frost, A. 1987 "Towards Australia" In *Australians to 1788.* Broadway: Fairfax, Syme & Weldon. 370-389.

Perry, T. 1982 *The Discovery of Australia.* Melbourne.

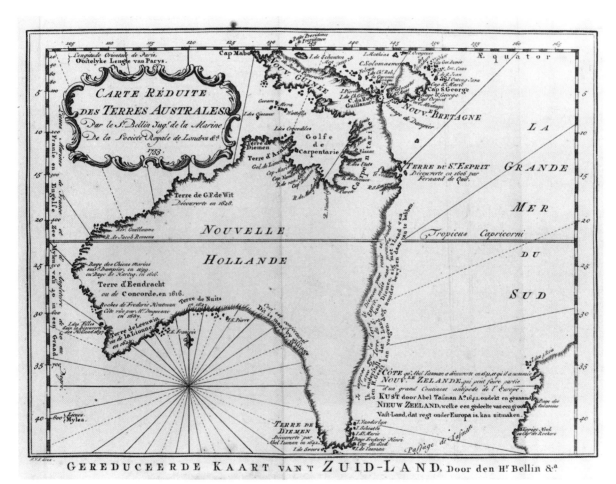

Figure 22. Map dated 1753 showing the state of knowledge prior to Cook's delineation of the coastline. Carpentaria is attached to New Guinea. (Ashmolean Museum)

Figure 23 above. Astronomical map of the Southern Hemisphere showing Terra Australis Incognita. In *Harmonia Macrocosmica* by A. Celar, Amsterdam 1661. (Museum of the History of Science)

Figure 24. Pocket Globes illustrating increasing knowledge of Australia in the second half of the 18th century.
left: c. 1750-60 by John Senex. Carpentaria is attached to New Guinea.
right: c.1790 the coast line is fully delineated except for the Bass Strait. The case lid contains a celestial map. (Museum of the History of Science)

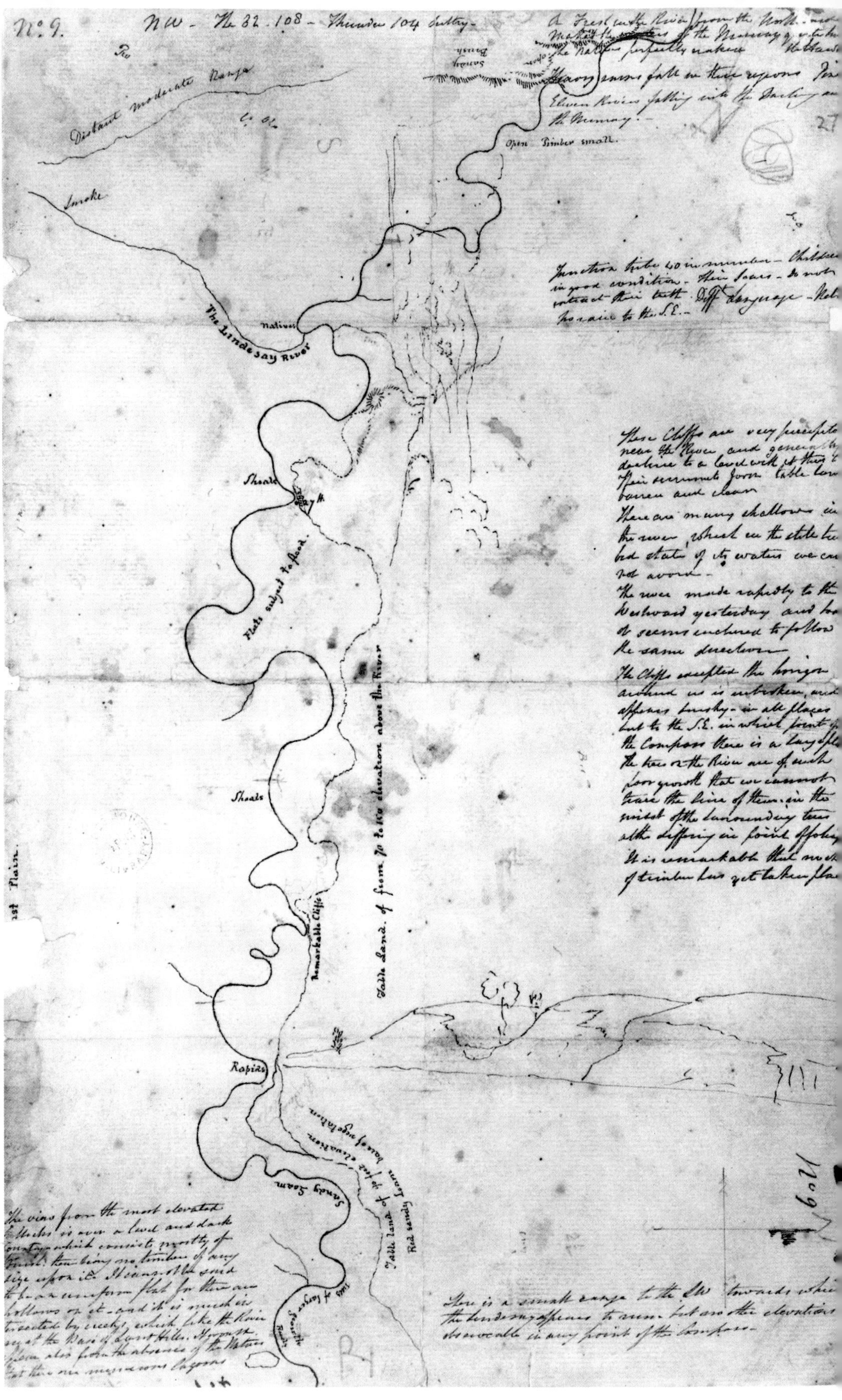

Figure 25.
One of a series of
sketch maps of
the Murray River
made by Sturt,
1830. (Rhodes
House Library Ms
Austral.s.4.fol.27)

20

4. Sturt and his Journeys

by Catherine Hart

In Rhodes House Library, Oxford, is an extremely valuable collection of the papers of Captain Charles Sturt (1795–1869), Australian explorer. The collection includes many of his journals, charts and maps as well as sketches and paintings, all produced while on his various expeditions. The collection also contains extensive correspondence with his family, with government officials regarding his expeditions, and with Sir Ralph Darling, the Governor of New South Wales, to whom he was originally appointed as Military Secretary when he arrived in Sydney in May 1827. These papers provide a very valuable insight into the impressions of one of the first European explorers in Australia.

Initially sent to Sydney guarding convicts, 'the father of Australian exploration'[1] went to New South Wales 'highly prejudiced against it, both from the nature of the service and the character of the great body of its inhabitants.'[2] Finding garrison life routine, he eagerly volunteered, and was appointed by Darling, to be leader of an expedition into the interior 'to ascertain the level of the inland plains, and to determine the supposed existence of an inland sea,'[3] a theory first proposed by Flinders and which many believed to be true. To Mr Alexander McLeay, Colonial Secretary for New South Wales, he wrote (1828): 'I anticipate that I shall come upon a Mediterranean Sea...I shall not be surprised if I find *Salt* water before I get many miles Northward.'[4]

Thus began a series of expeditions into the interior, which were particularly noteworthy for the discovery and mapping of several rivers. Again to the Colonial Secretary, he wrote: 'I am

Figure 26. Charles Sturt, c.1865. (Rhodes House Library Ms.Austral.s.5.d)

most anxious to determine the fate of the Macquarie...'[5] After penetrating the marshes of the Macquarie, and crossing vast plains, Sturt discovered the Darling.

In his official report to the Colonial Secretary regarding his second and probably most celebrated expedition (1830), Sturt explains how he availed himself 'of the opportunity to distinguish the River by the name of the "Murray"' (after Sir George Murray, then Colonial Secretary); how he named the "Lindesay" and

[1] A Short Account of the Public Life and Discoveries in Australia of Captain Sturt, [1869].

[2] Sturt, Mrs Napier George (1899). *Life of Charles Sturt.* London: Smith, Elder & Co., p. 22.

[3] Letter to Isaac Wood (10.11.1827) in Sturt, Mrs N. G. *Life of Charles Sturt.* London: Smith, Elder & Co., p. 24.

[4] Letter to A. McLeay, 6 Nov 1828. RHL *Sturt Papers,* Vol.1, s.4, no.2.

[5] Letter to Col. Sec., 4 Nov 1828. RHL *Sturt Papers,* Vol. 1, s.4, no.1.

Lake "Alexandrina"[6] (named so in honour of the young princess then heiress to the throne of Britain – later changed to Lake Victoria).

This second expedition left him very weak and nearly blind. He returned to England to seek advice and finally, in 1833, left the army. In 1834 he married Charlotte Green and returned to Australia to settle in New South Wales. Eager to return to exploration, Sturt traced the Hume to the Murray, while in charge of a drove of cattle for South Australia, in 1838.

In 1839 Sturt began an official career, accepting the post of Surveyor-General of South Australia, only to find that the British government had appointed someone else to the office. He was then offered the post of Assistant Commissioner, which he was not happy with, though he accepted it and executed it well. He recounted to Lady Darling four years later: '. . .it was an appointment I would not have accepted if it had

[6] Report to Col. Sec., 23 July 1830. RHL *Sturt Papers,* Vol. 1, s.4, no.8.

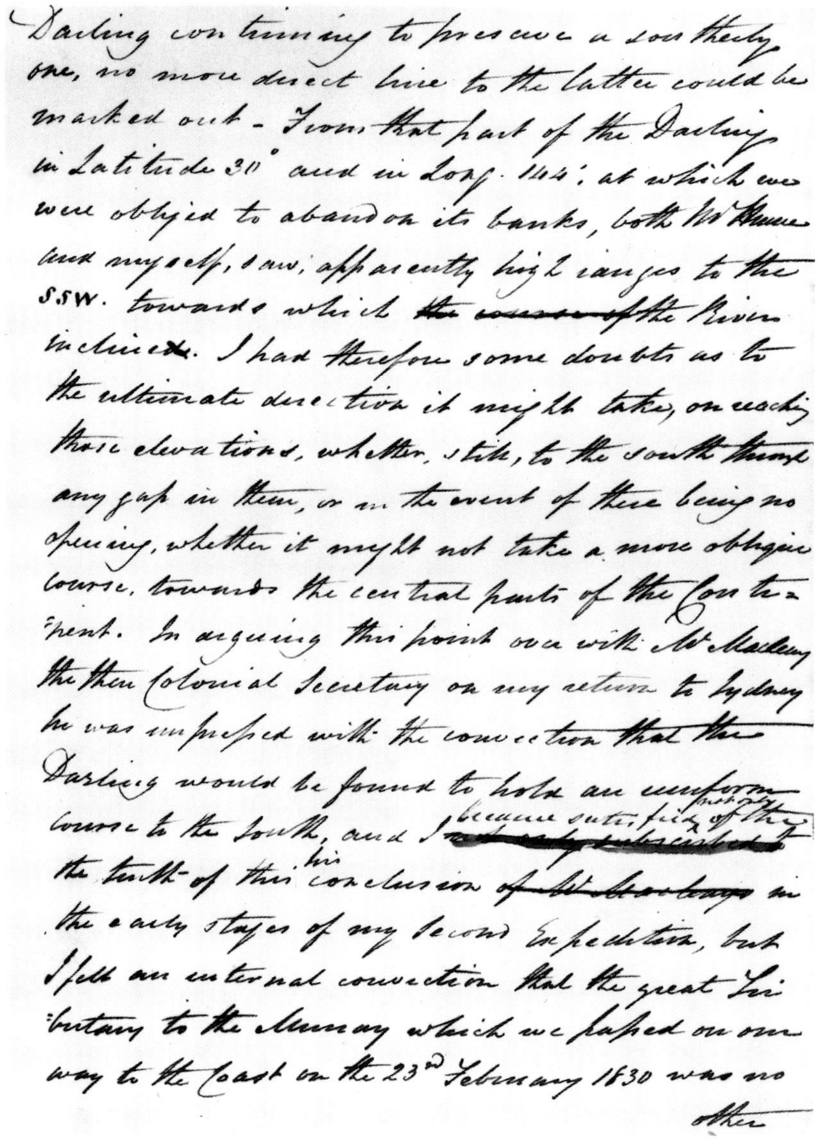

Figure 27.
Page from Sturt's 1844 Journal. (Rhodes House Library Ms.Austral.s.4*fol.102)

Figure 28 opposite.
Possum hunt, Murrumbidgee region, December 1829. Gouache on panel, after sketch made on his expedition. (Rhodes House Library Ms.Austral.s.5.d)

22

been first offered to me.'[7] Again it appears Sturt found this sort of life routine and longed for exploration again, as he explained to Lady Darling early in 1843: 'I am unhappy in my present position, and. . .would gladly do anything. . .to be employed in exploring central Australia. It would you will allow be a gigantic undertaking, but no one knows better than the General whether I am qualified for it or not. It was under his auspices I commenced my career as an Explorer, and it was under the guidance of Providence that I was more successful than any other. I should like to put the finishing stroke to the career I began in New South Wales by exploring the secrets of the Interior, and planting the Ensign of my country in the centre of this mysterious region.'[8]

Recommended by Sir Ralph Darling, who in a letter to Lord Stanley (then Secretary of State for the colonies) compares Sturt to Columbus: '. . .he appears urged on by fate – the result may be similar'[9] – Sturt received permission and equipment to begin his expedition to reach the centre of the continent.

In the journal kept during this expedition of 1844–5 we find the most interesting and detailed of Sturt's impressions of the Aborigines. His early descriptions (e.g. 1830), when he had as yet had very little contact with them, include references such as 'hostile Tribes', 'a treacherous and cruel race' and 'the lowest in the Scale of human beings'.[10] Fifteen years and two expeditions later,

[7] Letter to Lady Darling, 26 Jan 1843. RHL *Sturt Papers*, Vol.2, s.5, no.26.
[8] *ibid.*

[9] Letter from Darling to Lord Stanley, 7 Sept 1843. RHL *Sturt Papers*, Vol.2, s.5, no.27.
[10] Report to Col. Sec., 23 July 1830. RHL *Sturt Papers*, Vol.1, s.4, no.8.

Figure 29. Aboriginal camp, c.1830. Watercolour. (Rhodes House Library Ms.Austral.s.5.d)

Figure 30. Sturt's camp on the Murrumbidgee River, December 1829. Gouache on panel, after sketch made on his expedition. (Rhodes House Library Ms.Austral.s.5.d)

his attitude had changed markedly, as revealed in the following journal entry:

'He was exceedingly clean in his person, unobtrusive tho [sic] so much with us, and always respectful. I took a great fancy to this old man, and treated him with marked attention, and when I left the Camp to go to the Northwest, he came up to me as I was mounting my horse and embraced me by putting his arms over my shoulders, and bowed down his head to my breast.'[11]

His final attitude regarding the Aborigines might best be summed up by an entry which appears in the latter part of this journal: '. . . the Natives of this Country can be passed without much difficulty or danger. It is on the manner in which they are treated that their conduct to you depends.'[12]

Sturt's journeys were significant in that they resulted in a general survey of the largest river system of Australia and the opening up of South Australia. He was also the first traveller, and for a long time the only one, to approach the centre of the continent.[13]

Though a celebrated figure of Australian history, Sturt did not achieve what he much desired. He often sought promotion and financial stability, but was thwarted in many attempts at both. He became colonial secretary in 1849 after other official appointments, but held the post only until the end of 1851 when he retired on a pension granted by the colony. Four applications to be governor – of South Australia, Victoria, Queensland and Tasmania[14] – were all refused. In 1869 he was nominated K.C.M.G., but died without receiving that honour.

Although the worth of his character has recently been disputed (cf. Beale 1979) his impressions of Australia as an artist and explorer, contained in this collection of papers, are still an invaluable representation of early European explorers' ideas about the continent.

[11] Journal 1844-5, p. 69. RHL *Sturt Papers,* Journal s.4.
[12] *ibid.,* p. 243.

[13] *The Dictionary of National Biography* [-1917] Vol.19, pp. 136-7.
[14] Beale, Edgar (1979), *Sturt, the Chipped Idol.* Sydney: Sydney University Press, p. 3.

Figure 31. Unidentified aboriginal camp, probably Murray River region, c.1829-30. Gouache on panel, after sketch made on his expedition. (Rhodes House Library Ms.Austral.s.5.d)

5. Representation and Reality: Science and the Visual Image

by Elizabeth Edwards

The European exploration of Australia presented the scientist with major new fields of investigation, geographical, geological, botanical, zoological and anthropological. Rigorous scientific investigation, such as that developing at Oxford and elsewhere in the 19th century, is dependent on verifiable and quantifiable data, and from early on the visual image was an important source of information, supplementing descriptive accounts and collections of specimens. Photography, one of the most far-reaching inventions of the 19th century, became an important source of visual representation of the continent quite early in Australian history. The development of photography coincided with the later exploration of the interior of Australia and consolidation of colonial settlement, and it played an important role in reinforcing perceptions of the continent.

It was the documentary possibilities of photography which were most exciting to contemporaries and science was central to their concerns:

"It is to science, however, that photography, the child of science, renders and will increasingly render, the most valuable aid ... Hitherto the man of science, in many departments, has been at the mercy of the unscientific traveller. The ethnologist, the historian, the antiquarian, and often the geologist have to form theories upon data which have been gathered by a gleaner whose appreciation of the value of minute accuracy maybe inadequate" (*Quarterly Review*, 1864) This documentary role was paramount in Australia, for the primary purpose of exploration was the gathering of knowledge, which, through the demystification of the continent, would bring it subtly within the European's grasp. Photography was in some ways equated with civilization, which in 19th century terms was largely defined by science and technology. Indeed *Photographic*

News commented in 1861 that:

"No expedition of a civilizing tendency is now considered complete without the aid of photography"

Underlying this enthusiasm was the belief in the accuracy and reality of photographic recording:

"the photographer is bound by simple truth – happily that is an important, if not the all important principle in representation, he [the photographer] can neither adorn his picture, nor remove anything that is offensive ... appearing as the exact transcript of nature" (Bourne 1859)

This view is somewhat over-enthusiastic, even by contemporary standards, but as such it does capture a justifiable spirit of scientific and objective optimism in the medium and gives an indication of the way in which photography was viewed by contemporaries.

However, photography, like other media, is rarely as objective as popular belief would have it but is intricately bound up with society's perception of the world around it. Photographs are at the same time representations of the world and sources of information about the world. As representations they present a view of the world which is dependent on the unconscious cultural values of both photographer and audience. It affects what is selected as significant and how it is interpreted. Consequently the objectivity of the photograph as a source of information must viewed within this framework. The dual aspect of photography had its antecedents in the paintings and engravings by which Australia was first presented to the European public. Most early representations of Australia had the same documentary purpose as photography and the movement from paintings and engravings to photography should be seen as a continuum in representation rather than as two entirely separate media.

The great scientific voyages of the late eighteenth century produced a wealth of visual images of Australia. Scientific draughtsmen were employed on the voyages to produce anything from coastal profiles to botanical studies (Smith 1960: 8–95). Such drawings and paintings were widely disseminated in the form of engravings and were extremely influential in forming European perceptions of Australia. There was intense interest amongst the educated classes in the natural history material being gathered during the early voyages and there was a demand for accurate depiction of specimens. However, although original drawings such as those of Parkinson were primarily documentary in purpose, when published and disseminated as engravings the Australian subjects were absorbed into the visual vocabulary of the late 18th century (Smith 1985: 27). Thomas Chambers' engraving from Parkinson's drawing, "Two of the Natives of New Holland Advancing in Combat" of 1773, presents the viewer with two classical heroic figures of more gladitorial than Australian appearance, one of whom carries a sword, equally classical in character. Another example is provided by Medland's engraving based on Cleveley's drawing of the Aborigines of Botany Bay which was published in 1789 in Governor Phillip's account of the first settlement . It has clear documentary intent; attention has been given to the construction of what is clearly a bark boat and to the shape of the shield, but the presentation of the figures and their facial characteristics are again purely classical [fig. 32]. Such

Figure 32. 'Natives of Botany Bay.' Engraving by T. Medland after a drawing by R. Cleveley, 1789.
(Pitt Rivers Museum)

Figure 33. 'North View of Sydney.' Aquatint by J. Lycett, 1824-25. (Ashmolean Museum)

representations can be attributed in part to the conventions of the late 18th century engraver's art which enhanced so many books of the period but they also represent a perception of the primitive, a vision of arcadia transplanted, which is integrally entwined with the enlightenment concept of the noble savage.

This image, however, was short lived, for its basis was as a literary and philosophical device rather than an actual observation of the "primitive" (Burrow 1968). By the 1820's and 30's representations of Australia were increasingly concerned with the growing stability and self-confidence of the colony rather than scientific

recording of specimens. Many of those published for wide dissemination in England were nonetheless still presented to appeal to an English audience and engage their sympathy for and identity with the Australian landscape (not to mention sell the engravings). Instances of this are Joseph Lycett's aquatints of New South Wales [fig. 33] published in 1824–25, which lost much of the directness and documentary accuracy of the originals when rendered in terms of the romantic picturesque (Dutton 1974:136–7) . Similarly, John Pye's engraving after Westall "Entrance to Port Lincoln taken from behind Memory Cove" whilst suggesting a vastness of landscape, has a "terrible beauty" reminiscent of contemporary picturesque views of the English Lake District [fig. 34]. Although much of the original scientific impetus had passed, some excellent sympathetic documentary paintings of the indigenous population were still produced, A fine example is the series of watercolours of Tasmanian Aborigines painted by Thomas Bock (1790–1855) in 1839 [fig. 35 & 36] for Lady Franklin, the Governor's wife (Plomley 1965). The Tasmanians are perhaps for the last time portrayed as young, healthy and vital individuals with an individual culture, accurately observed by the artist. The direct and unaffected nature of these paintings makes them both fine portraits and sensitive documents.

The changing emphasis in the representation of Australia and especially its Aboriginal population can be placed in the broader context of the way in which the developing colony saw itself. There was a growing identification with the land that had been colonised, but an identification which largely excluded the indigenous population. Aborigines ceased to be central to representations of Australian landscape, but became incidental to it, placed there as little more than

Figure 34. 'Entrance to Port Lincoln.' Engraving by J. Pye after a painting by M. Westall, 1814.
(Ashmolean Museum)

Figure 35 opposite. Manetargenna carrying firestick. Watercolour by Thomas Bock 1834. (Pitt Rivers Museum)

30

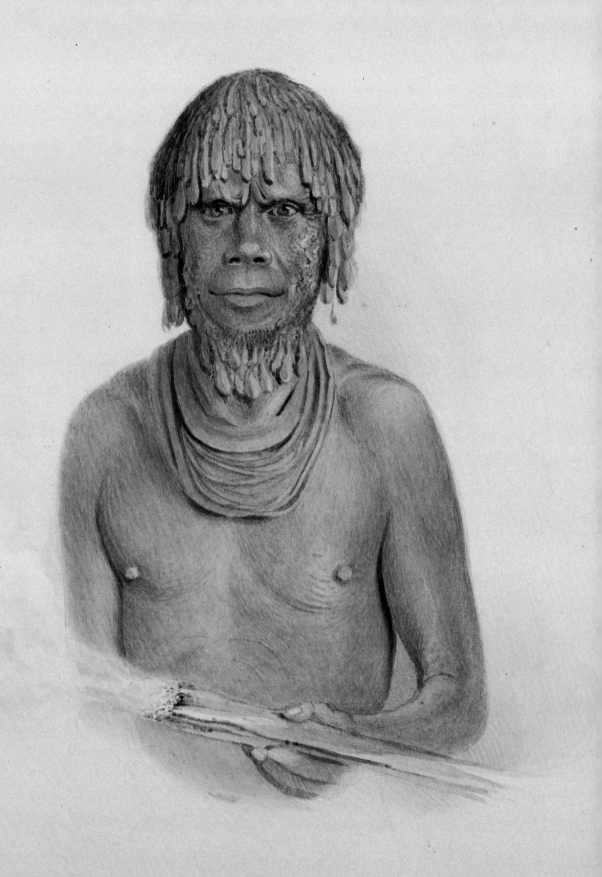

Figure 37. 'By water to Parramatta.' Engraving by J. Heath, 1798. (Ashmolean Museum)

"exotic reference" [fig. 37]. However shifting ideas on the nature of mankind were equally influential. Whereas the enlightenment view had been fundamentally "monogenist", considering all mankind capable of "civilization", the early years of the 19th century saw an increasing stress on the relationship between race and the capability of "civilization" (Stocking 1968:35–6). The growing dominance of evolutionary theory in science gave the weight of scientific truth to assumptions concerning the superiority of the white races. By the time photography rather than engraving became the most common medium for the mass dissemination of images, attitudes of both the producer and consumer of such images had changed radically.

Although early reports commented on surface similarities in landscape between England and eastern Australia, the realities of settlement were very different. From the very beginning there had been violent incidents between white settlers and the Aborigines. As the 19th century progressed and white incursions into the more productive hunting lands grew, so Aboriginal resistance developed to meet the gravity of the situation. Many incidents were based not on unreasoned ill-feeling on the part of either party, but rather on a series of fundamental mutual misunderstandings on such issues as concepts of land, property and reciprocity. The increasing number of violent incidents, particularly on the frontiers of white settlement caused the Abori-

Figure 36 opposite. Num-bloo-te (Jenny) Watercolour by Thomas Bock 1839 (Pitt Rivers Museum)

gines to become objects of fear, their violence being seen as an inherent attribute of their savagery (Reynolds 1983). The popular currency of these ideas had profound influence on the way in which Aborigines came to be represented. By the 1850's the Aboriginal population of Australia was widely regarded as degraded, primitive in the extreme, a remnant of the childhood of mankind and above all a dying race. But it was precisely for these reasons that the Australian Aborigines excited the scientific mind and much of Oxford's attention to Australia in the 19th century was in some way linked to these ideas.

Of all the photographic material on Australia collected as scientific data in Oxford, it is the anthropological record which is most substantial. This is not surprising, for anthropology and ethnology were central to the dominant evolutionary debate which Huxley described as "the question of questions for mankind – the problem which underlies all others" (Huxley 1906:52) . The fact that photography was perceived as presenting a greater "reality" than other media made it the ideal medium for collecting scientific data. Yet despite the potential of the medium the collection of such data was by no means systematic, but rather it involved the gathering of miscellaneous albums of images relating to a certain subject, somewhat in the 18th and early 19th century antiquarian's tradition of the portfolio of prints and drawings which could be used for study (Seiberling 1986:47–8). For example, Professor Arthur Thomson (Professor of Human Anatomy 1893–1934) possessed an album of assorted prints, drawings and photographs, including much Australian material, which had been shown at meetings of the Anthropological Society of London in 1867 [fig. 38]. A number of collections were made by scientists in Oxford during the 19th century including such various

Figure 38. Series of photographs by Charles Walters in the album of visual material shown at the Anthropological Society of London 1867. (Pitt Rivers Museum)

Figure 39. Prospectus sheet from Kerry's studio showing the range of images of Aborigines available for purchase, c.1890. (Pitt Rivers Museum)

disciplines as anthropology, astronomy, egyptology and anatomy: one suspects that there were more which have since been dispersed. The original Pitt Rivers donation included Australian crania which were accompanied by photographs of Aborigines. Interestingly enough these photographs were not ones made specifically for anthropological study but were studio portraits and cartes-de-visite which could be purchased at any Australian photographer's rooms [fig. 39]. Yet they were collected by men like E.B. Tylor and presented to Oxford as material of scientific interest. The albums of photographs [fig. 40] collected by Professor Moseley on the H.M.S. Challenger scientific expedition (1872–6) exemplify this and include a wide variety of material

ranging from the official expedition photographs of natural history to cartes-de-visite showing tableaux of "Aboriginal life".

There was however intellectual justification for this apparently haphazard accumulation of material. The objectification of the indigenous population, both physically and culturally, as specimens for scientific investigation was legitimated by society's broader beliefs concerning the nature of race. There was no point to be proven, merely one to illustrate, for the "primitiveness" of the Aborigines was not in question. All photographs of Australian Aborigines were, in broad terms therefore, of scientific interest, a view which is certainly borne out by contemporary comment, whether it be learned

Group of Australian Natives on the Richmond River N.S.Wales near the boundry of Queensland.

The small photographs are of Natives of Maryborough Queensland.

Figure 40. Photographs from various Australian commercial photographers collected by Prof. Moseley, c. 1870-75. (Department of Zoology)

institutions or exhibition reviews.

One of the driving forces in the collection of photographic images in the second half of the 19th century was the idea that the Aborigines were a "dying race". Aboriginal society was viewed as degraded and totally lacking in social dynamic, thus its extinction was, by evolutionary process, inevitable. Images of Aborigines were intended precisely to capture the "reality" before it was too late. Despite pressure from scientists such as T.H. Huxley, however, no systematic survey to record the supposedly "dying race" was ever undertaken, indeed the *British Journal of Photography* was moved to comment on the Australian case when reviewing the photo-

graphic contributions at the Sydney International Exhibition in 1879:

"It is a great pity that the governments of those countries who employ photographers largely do not secure, for once and for all, as good a collection as can be made of the original races, which are rapidly dying out. These collections would not only form a very interesting record for the country and future generations but would be valued extremely by the scientific world in Europe and elsewhere; . . . it [is] a great pity – nay, a fault – not to embrace this last opportunity afforded of perpetuating the pictorial records of the races that once peopled this great country of the future, independent of the valuable impetus and service it would render to ethnological research, which at this moment, is one of the topics of the age" (Hart 1879)

This comment not only states the scientific standpoint but also indicates the growing confidence and sense of future of the colony. Indeed, the concept of the "dying race", like that of *terra nullis*, provided some justification for white settlement and exploitation of Australian land. The juxtaposition of the new, civilized, progressive and living against the old, primitive, stagnant and dying was expressed photographically. Photographic firms such as Bayliss or Kerry & King sold photographs which stressed the modernity of the colony for European consumption, views of Government House over neat lawns, the vision of orderliness, the modern metropolitan buildings of the cities or the peaceful reverie of a fisherman on the Hawksbury River [fig. 41 & 42]. Whereas photographs of the aboriginal population , were little more than an aspect of the exotica which Australia had to offer.

Looking more closely at some of the types of photographs collected it becomes apparent that the material cannot be easily categorized. Some photographs were certainly taken primarily for the "scientific study" of the Aboriginal population, for they are concerned with the measurement of the subject's body in response to the need for precise data which could be fitted into contemporary classificatory and evolutionary schemes. The subject was placed against a plain background with a measuring rod and photographed, usually full face and profile, so that the physical details were clearly visible . The recording of the body as a scientific specimen symbolised the way in which the indigenous population was, by the second half of the 19th century viewed as an object of scientific curiosity, isolated

Figure 41. Hawksbury River, New South Wales. Photograph by King Studios, c.1880-85. (Pitt Rivers Museum)

Figure 42. Melbourne Exhibition Hall, 1885. (Pitt Rivers Museum)

from cultural context. The photographs by Paul Foelsche, taken in Northern Territories in the early 1870's, are good examples of this genre [fig. 43]. By the 1860's and 1870's this kind of photograph had become the accepted "ethnographic mode" not only in Australia but elsewhere. However, as a mode of representation it was not restricted to narrow anthropological and ethnological contexts but influenced photographs taken for quite different purposes. An interesting example of this is the series of photographs of Tasmanian aboriginals taken by Charles Woolley in 1866 [fig. 44a & b]. At one level they are fine portrait photographs, but the treatment of the subjects, the decontextualized full face and profile, is overt acknowledgement of the scientific interest of the subjects. Henry Balfour, first Curator of the Pitt Rivers Museum, purchased a set of prints of Woolley's photographs and the 1858 series attributed to Bishop Nixon [fig. 45a &

b] from the Hobart photographer J.W.Beattie. For him they fitted into the tradition of collecting visual material to augment scientific data. Both Balfour and Tylor were interested in the Tasmanians as living examples of the last remnants of Palaeolithic man. The photographs and the Bock watercolours were used as visual material in displays of Tasmanian artifacts in the Pitt Rivers Museum for many years. Another more direct scientific application of Woolley's photographs were the tracings made of the profiles of Patty, Wapperty, Bill Lanney and others as evidence in the debate over the racial identity of surviving Tasmanians (Ling Roth 1898).

It was in the context of the "dying race" that the noble savage made a comeback. Again, Woolley's portraits can be interpreted in this light for the heads are framed in misty vignettes, fading out both literally and metaphorically. Indeed "last of ..." was not an infrequent cap-

38

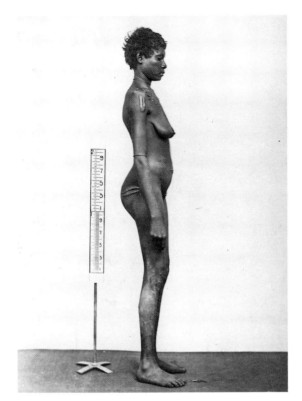
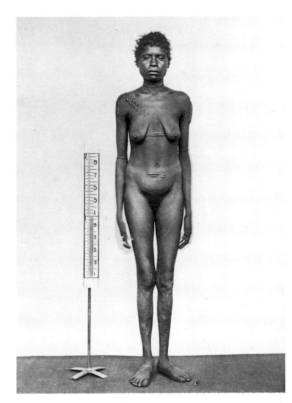

Figure 43. Physical Anthropology specimens. Photographs by Paul Foelsche, early 1870's. (Pitt Rivers Museum)

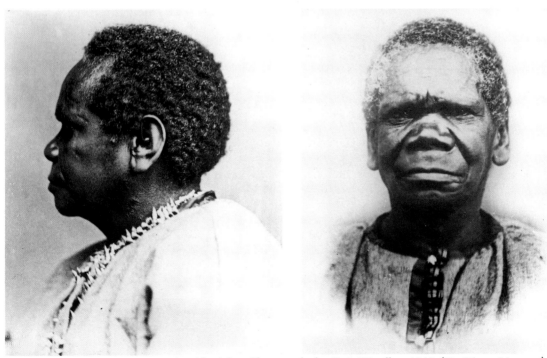

Figure 44. Patty, Tasmanian Aborigine. Photographs by C. A. Woolley, 1866. (Pitt Rivers Museum)

tion applied to these and other images of the indigenous population (Maynard 1985:100–102). Amongst the most celebrated images in this genre were the studio portraits of Aborigines by a photographer of German origin, J.W. Lindt (1845–1926). The series of Clarence River people, taken in the early 1870's, depict the subject, surrounded by items of material culture (often in somewhat incongruous mixtures), against a back drop of a soft romantic landscape [fig. 46 & 47]. Although the images are powerfully sympathetic and statuesque, it is the sympathy of romantic sentiment for a "dying race". These sentiments are echoed in the still lethargy, the sense of resignation, which subfuses the images, when compared, for instance, with the vitality of the Tasmanians painted by Bock. Despite the highly constructed nature of Lindt's images, contemporaries described them as the "first successful attempt at representing the native

blacks truthfully as well as artistically" (Davies & Stanbury 1985:72) suggesting that they fulfilled contemporary perceptions of the Aboriginal race. As such it is not surprising that these were widely disseminated images, a number of sets survive in "scientific" collections in Britain (including Oxford) and elsewhere, for the scientific view of the destiny of the native Australians was an integral part of the popular perception.

Less "noble" were the carte-de-visite photographs which were the mass-market photographs of the 1860's and 1870's. In a way similar to picture postcards, which disseminated very similar images a generation later, these little photographs, such as those in Moseley's albums, were produced in very many thousands and were an integral part of the popular image of Aborigines (Peterson 1985). They are still, nevertheless, manifestations of the same set of values which produced Lindt's images, but their lack of aes-

Figure 45 above and opposite. Tasmanians at Oyster Cove Settlement. Photographs attributed to Bishop Nixon, 1858.
(Pitt Rivers Museum)

Figures 46-47. The Noble Savage. Studio photographs of Clarence River Aborigines by J. W. Lindt, early 1870's. (Pitt Rivers Museum)

Figure 47.

thetic finesse is in many cases closely associated with a lack of sympathy for and observation of the subject. The majority of these photographs are either "types" in the "ethnographic mode" or constructed genre pieces showing aspects of Aboriginal culture. At this date there are relatively few "field" images as such because of the technical difficulties involved. The models for these "recontextualized" cultural interpretations were often Aborigines who had moved to the fringes of the large cites such as Melbourne and Adelaide, posed in a way to reinforce European perceptions. In some way these images could be interpreted as defusing fears about the Aborigines. The very traits which Europeans found alarming were codified. Physical peculiarities, symbols of primitiveness such as weapons (indicating savagery) and skin clothing or aggressive stances, were reduced from the threatening to the amusing when encapsulated within the frame of the image in the photographer's studio [fig. 48]. Yet images of this nature were collected by scientists as the quantity of them found in the collections of museums , universities and learned institutions testifies.

The ill-defined boundaries of what was and was not considered "scientific" reflects not only the fact that the production of most visual material was outside the control of those who sought to use it as data but also in imprecise ideas as to exactly what that data should be. How to express culture visually in an objective way is a question which vexes anthropologists to this day. This hesitancy of purpose has however resulted in a wide range of Australian material being gathered together in Oxford although perhaps its potential was never fully realized. Anthropologists had gradually, throughout the 19th century, improved both the quality and quantity of their data. Visual material was an integral part of this: Henry Balfour writing to his friend Baldwin Spencer in Melbourne in 1898 specifically asked for photographic material on Australia saying:

"Photos. I find are so important an adjunct to a museum that I try to beg all I can for a series I am making for the Museum" (Spencer Ms.)

In later years visual material, perhaps inevitably, came to be regarded as ephemeral because it lacked that very structure which was associated with modern scientific method. Nevertheless the influence of photography and its precursors, the 18th and early 19th century engraving, in both moulding and perpetuating European ideas of Australia should not be underestimated. The underlying theme that links these together is the gathering of knowledge and the wide dissemination of images which is fundamental to changing

Figure 48.   Carte-de-Visite photograph suggesting aggression, c.1865-70. (Pitt Rivers Museum)

perceptions and understanding of Australia. Even today images of one sort or another are the only perception of Australia experienced by many Europeans: paintings, engravings and early photographs represent merely the first layers of a continuing process.

REFERENCES

Bourne,S. 1859 "On Some Requisites Necessary for the Production of the Good Photograph". *Photographic News* iii:308.

Burrow, J.W. 1968 *Evolution and Society: a Study in Victorian Social Theory*. Cambridge: University Press.

Davies, A. & Stanbury, P. 1985 *The Mechanical Eye in Australia, Photography 1841–1900*. Melbourne: Oxford University Press.

Dutton, G. 1974 *White on Black: The Australian Aboriginal in Art*. Sydney: Macmillan.

Hart, L. 1879 "The Sydney International Exhibition". *British Journal of Photography* (28 November) XXV:572–573.

Huxley, T. H. 1906 "On the Relation of Man to the Lower Animals". In *Man's Place in Nature and other Essays*, 52–110. London: Dent.

Ling Roth, H. 1898 "Is Mrs. F.C.Smith the 'Last'?". *Journal of the Anthropological Institute* XXVII:451–454.

Lycett, J. 1824 *Views in Australia*. London: J.Souter.

Maynard, M. 1985 "Projections of Melancholy" In I.Donaldson & T.Donaldson (eds.) *Seeing the First Australians*. 92–109. Sydney: Allen & Unwin.

Parkinson, S. 1784 *A Journal of a Voyage to the South Seas*. London: Stanfield Parkinson.

Peterson, N. 1985 "The Popular Image" In I.Donaldson & T.Donaldson (eds.) *Seeing the First Australians* , 164–180. Sydney: Allen & Unwin.

Phillip, A. 1789 *The Voyage of Governor Phillip to Botany Bay with an account of the Establishment of the Colonies of Port Jackson and Norfolk Islands*. London: J.Stockdale.

Plomley, N.J.B. 1965 "Thomas Bock's Water-colours of the Tasmanian Aborigines" *Records of the Queen Victoria Museum, Launceston, N.S.18*

Photographic News 1861 5:120

Quarterly Review 1864 Quoted in *Journal of the Royal Photographic Society* (15 November) 1864.

Reynolds, H. 1983 *The Other Side of the Frontier*. Ringwood: Pelican Australia.

Seiberling, G. 1986 *Amateurs, Photography and the Mid-Victorian Imagination*. Chicago: University Press.

Smith,B. 1960 *European Vision and the South Seas 1768–1850*. London: Oxford University Press.

1985 "The First European Depictions" In I.Donaldson & T.Donaldson (eds.) *Seeing the First Australians* , 21–34. Sydney: Allen & Unwin.

Stocking, G. 1968 *Race, Evolution and Culture*. New York: Free Press.

Pukamani

The objects illustrated on these pages are used in the Pukamani mortuary rituals of the Tiwi of Melville and Bathurst Islands. The posts are positioned around the grave of the deceased as a memorial. The baskets are used to store food in the ceremony and are sometimes broken or jammed on top of the posts. H. K. Fry who made this collection was an Australian medical practitioner and one of the early students for the Diploma in Anthropology at Oxford.

All objects and Aboriginal artefacts illustrated in this book are in the collections of the Pitt Rivers Museum.

Figure 49. N. TERRITORY – MELVILLE ISLAND
Pukamani poles.
Collected and donated by H. K. Fry
1915.10.23-25

Figure 50. N. TERRITORY – MELVILLE ISLAND
Bag made of stringy-bark
Collected and donated by H. K. Fry
1915.10.20

Figure 51. N. TERRITORY – MELVILLE ISLAND
Bag made of stringy-bark
Collected and donated by H. K. Fry
1915.10.19

Figure 52. N. TERRITORY – MELVILLE ISLAND
Armlet of stringy-bark
Collected and donated by H. K. Fry
1917.6.29

Figure 53. N. TERRITORY – MELVILLE ISLAND
Armlet of stringy-bark
Collected and donated by H. K. Fry

6. The Original Australians and the Evolution of Anthropology

by Howard Morphy

The collection of Australian Aboriginal art and artefacts in the Pitt Rivers Museum is important for what it symbolises about the place of Aborigines in the history of anthropology, and about their place in Australian society for much of the twentieth century. Almost the entire collection of Australian objects dates from before the First World War. Why were Aborigines so interesting then and so neglected subsequently? Was there something about their material culture that made European museums lose interest in it for a generation or more or did its neglect reflect something about European attitudes to Aborigines? The situation is even more puzzling with hindsight, since today the arts of Arnhem Land and Central Australia are acknowledged to be

among the world's great living artistic traditions, and museums are striving to fill the gaps in their collections created by those missing years.

In the nineteenth century Australian Aborigines were at the heart of theories of social evolution, and items of their material culture accumulated in ethnographic collections around the world as examples of the products of early stages of human development. At its beginning anthropology accepted the social evolutionary theory that followed on from Darwin's insights into the world of nature, and that for a time imposed a rigid way of looking at human culture. The Pitt Rivers Museum and Oxford were at the centre of these early views but were also part of the process that ultimately led to the

Figure 54. W. AUSTRALIA – HAMERSLEY
Club or throwing-stick
Collected by and purchased from E. Clement
1898.75.12

Figure 55. N. TERRITORY – ARANDA OR NEIGHBOURING TRIBE
Boomerang
Collected by the Spencer-Gillen Expedition 1901-2
Donated by W. Baldwin Spencer
1903.39.63

Figure 56. W. AUSTRALIA
Boomerang
Collected by and purchased from E. Clement
1898.75.35

simple social evolutionary schema being abandoned through the development of modern anthropology.

Many of the Aboriginal artefacts in the Pitt Rivers Museum were part of the original gift to the University made in 1884. The objects Pitt Rivers gave, and the order he imposed on them, made them no neutral assemblage but the embodiment of a theory. He ordered his collection typologically to show the formal and functional relationships between objects in space and time (see Chapman 1985). His assumption was that culture had evolved in small steps through the modification of existing ideas and that eventually the accumulation of these small changes resulted in major transformations. As far as objects were concerned cumulative changes led to a diversification of types of objects within a set and eventually to the production of objects with increased complexity. Material culture provided a model for the development of other aspects of culture, for religious and for political institutions (Chapman 1985:33). The implication of the model was that societies with simple material culture were at a stage of development associated with equivalently simple religious institutions and political systems. He even implied that human languages could likewise be arranged on a hierarchy of evolutionary development, with societies which possessed simple technologies also having simple languages:

'These Australian shields are called Wadna, and some idea of the slight value which aboriginal names afford as conveying a correct idea of the thing named may be formed from the circumstance that on seeing for the first time an English boat they called it Wadna, from its resemblance to their shields.'

Lane-Fox (Pitt Rivers) 1874:7

In Pitt Rivers' model of the world the Australian Aborigines were important as they

Figure 57. S. AUSTRALIA –
NARRINJERI TRIBE
Boomerang
Collected by H. Balfour 1914
Balfour Gift
1938.35.1346

Figure 58. N. NEW SOUTH
WALES
Boomerang
Hardy Collection: probably collected
by H. Stockdale
Donated by R. F. Wilkins
1900.55.112

Figure 59. N. TERRITORY –
ARANDA OR NEIGHBOURING
TRIBE
Boomerang
Collected by the Spencer-Gillen
Expedition 1901-2
Donated by W. Baldwin Spencer
1903.39.61

49

were thought to be living representatives of earlier stages of human culture – people left behind. The Aborigines had in his terms a simple material culture; one in which representative objects from the early developmental stages of many artefact types could be found. Beginning with Australia and working outwards he constructed diagrams that moved from simple to more complex stages in the development of forms. His diagram of the development of clubs, shields, boomerangs and lances, all from an original simple straight stick is a brilliant representation of his model (cf. Chapman 1985:32).

The model was being developed at the height of Victorian self-confidence when European civilisation seemed to be the peak of human achievement, and it made the colonial enterprise part of a natural evolutionary process. Strong nations survived and prospered while the weak died out. People existing in the nineteenth century with stone age cultures were seen as survivals from a past era, doomed to extinction through contact with a superior race. The proclaimed extinction of the Tasmanian Aborigines, strenuously denied in recent years by their descendants, fitted neatly into the schema.

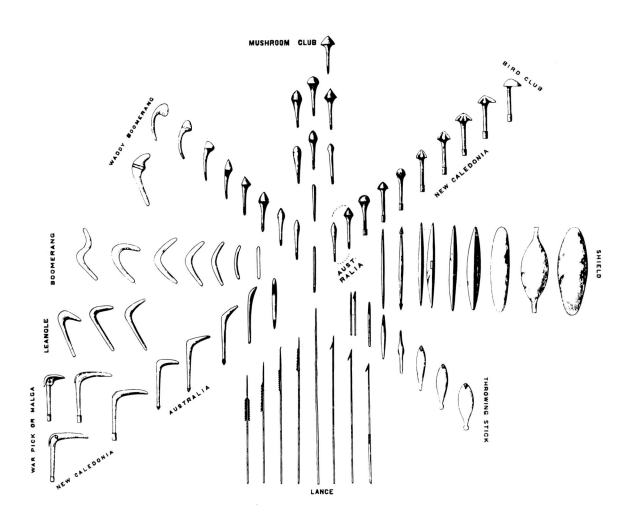

Figure 60. 'Clubs, Boomerangs, Shields and Lances' an illustration from *The Evolution of Culture,* 1875.

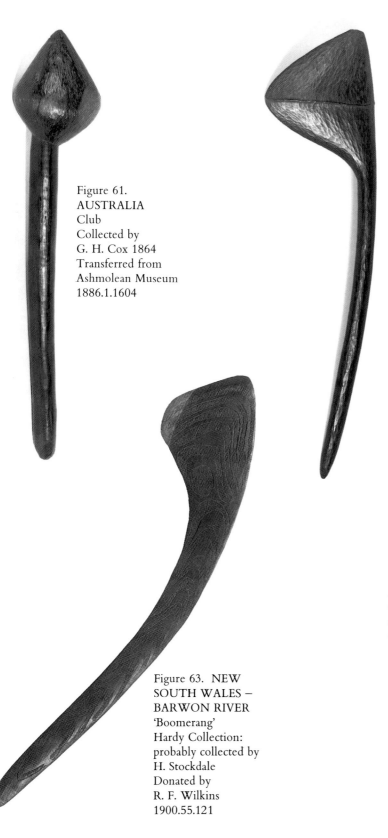

Figure 61.
AUSTRALIA
Club
Collected by
G. H. Cox 1864
Transferred from
Ashmolean Museum
1886.1.1604

Figure 62.
AUSTRALIA
Club
Original Pitt Rivers
Collection
1884.12.300

Figure 63. NEW
SOUTH WALES –
BARWON RIVER
'Boomerang'
Hardy Collection:
probably collected by
H. Stockdale
Donated by
R. F. Wilkins
1900.55.121

Figure 64.
AUSTRALIA
Club
Original Pitt Rivers
Collection
1884.12.81

Material culture became a sign and an explanation: a sign of the state of savagery of people and an explanation of their demise. The preconceptions of the simple evolutionary theorists made an objective study of Aboriginal society almost

Figure 65. VICTORIA
Spear-thrower
Collected by John Sanderson before 1871
Donated by Rev. Finlay Sanderson
1952.3.7

impossible, for the theory masked contradictions in the reality. It was not necessary to examine how it was that the Tasmanians died when their death was considered inevitable. Neither was it necessary to prove that Australian religious

beliefs were as simple as their material culture; the relationship between the two was assumed in advance. Material culture was a sign of mental culture.

As a consequence of this, the inevitable course of history, morality did not have to concern itself with solutions but with palliatives; in that memorable phrase, Christian duty was to 'smooth the pillow of the dying race'.

The model was a consequence of a too literal application of Darwinian theory to human societies, rather than some Machiavellian attempt to justify colonialism. Indeed the typologising of Pitt Rivers contained within it the seeds of a radically different view of the relationships between cultures, and was an early attempt to view social evolution in a systematic way. Pitt Rivers' typological approach was inherently reflexive, showing analogies between peoples across the world and providing the possibility of seeing similarities as well as differences. Eventually it would be seen that everything did not progress together in neat unilinear stages, that different aspects of culture were frequently out of step with each other and that the stages that were identified were an imposition on the typology rather than something that arose out of it. At some stage in the future the typological ordering of Pitt Rivers' collection would provide a productive context for reflecting on the unity and diversity of human kind. During his lifetime it served more to separate people out.

When the Pitt Rivers collection was moved to Oxford, unilinear evolution was still the dominant theory and was the one followed by the leading British anthropologists of the time, Sir Edward Tylor and Sir James Frazer. Under the conditions of the Pitt Rivers bequest Tylor had been appointed to lecture on anthropology in the University Museum and it was Tylor and H.N. Moseley, the Linacre Professor of Anatomy, who organised the removal of the collection to Oxford. Among those employed to carry out the move and label the objects was a young biology graduate, Baldwin Spencer. Spencer was to play a leading role in the

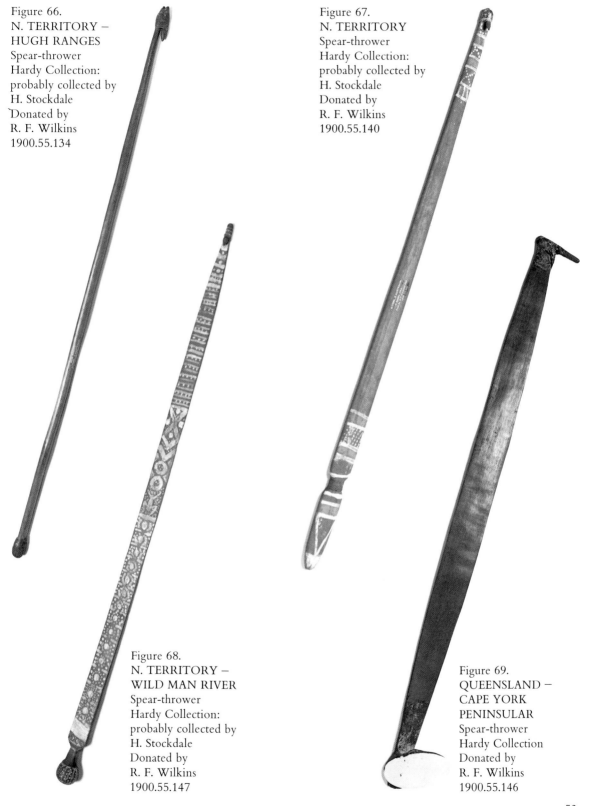

Figure 66.
N. TERRITORY –
HUGH RANGES
Spear-thrower
Hardy Collection:
probably collected by
H. Stockdale
Donated by
R. F. Wilkins
1900.55.134

Figure 67.
N. TERRITORY
Spear-thrower
Hardy Collection:
probably collected by
H. Stockdale
Donated by
R. F. Wilkins
1900.55.140

Figure 68.
N. TERRITORY –
WILD MAN RIVER
Spear-thrower
Hardy Collection:
probably collected by
H. Stockdale
Donated by
R. F. Wilkins
1900.55.147

Figure 69.
QUEENSLAND –
CAPE YORK
PENINSULAR
Spear-thrower
Hardy Collection
Donated by
R. F. Wilkins
1900.55.146

establishment of modern anthropology even though to the end of his life he too stuck to the evolutionary model he had inherited from his teachers. The opportunity for him to make a contribution to anthropology began with his acceptance in 1887 of the Chair of Biology at Melbourne University.

'I know of course that thanks to opportunities that come to few workers, I have been able to do some good anthropological work and the capacity to do this I owe to Moseley and Tylor. It was just the merest chance that when I was demonstrating for Moseley the Pitt Rivers collection was left to the university . . . for a month I was with Moseley and Tylor [packing it up] and from both of them but specially the latter I learnt so much.'
Letter from Spencer to Balfour, 6.1.1903, P.R.M. Archives

Spencer's introduction to Australian Aboriginal culture was as a member of the Horn Scientific Expedition to Central Australia in 1894. Spencer travelled as the expedition's biologist, the anthropological work being in the hands of Sir Edward Stirling, the director of the South Australian Museum. But the anthropological event of real significance was the meeting of Spencer with Frank Gillen at Alice Springs on the 15th of July. Gillen had spent many years in Central Australia and was the postmaster at Alice Springs as well as the local magistrate and Protector of Aborigines. He had over the years become interested in Aboriginal culture and made a large collection of Aboriginal artefacts. Although Spencer had shown an interest in Aborigines before his meeting with Gillen, that meeting must have opened out further the possibilities of research to him. It must have helped considerably that they established an immediate personal rapport.

Mulvaney and Calaby (1985) have argued that it was probably in preparing the Horn manuscript for publication that Spencer began to move the focus of his research from animals to people. He found Stirling's report woefully inadequate

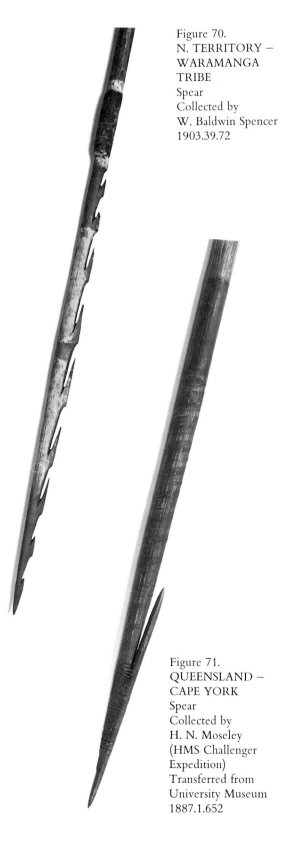

Figure 70.
N. TERRITORY –
WARAMANGA
TRIBE
Spear
Collected by
W. Baldwin Spencer
1903.39.72

Figure 71.
QUEENSLAND –
CAPE YORK
Spear
Collected by
H. N. Moseley
(HMS Challenger
Expedition)
Transferred from
University Museum
1887.1.652

54

and was persuaded by Gillen's knowledge and enthusiasm that there was far more to be understood than had ever been written.

Until this point in time anthropology had been carried out largely from the armchair, with theorists basing their work either on formal interviews in unfamiliar environments or most often on the replies to questionnaires sent out to missionaries, planters or government officials stationed in distant places. The questionnaire method produced lists of customs and practices that obscured the complexities of social life and made them grist for the same typological mill that ground out hierarchical sequences of artefacts. The collaboration between Spencer and Gillen brought into being modern fieldwork methods in anthropology. It was not simply a question of long term association with the group being studied. What was new was long term data-gathering in the field informed by theory and guided by some perception of scientific method. Until Spencer and Gillen the theorists had largely been separated from the data; Spencer enabled the two to be brought together.

Initially the actual data-gathering was done by Gillen, but later Spencer himself undertook major expeditions with him. But though it was Gillen who early on asked most of the questions, the questions were formulated through his correspondence with Spencer; a correspondence that had a warmth, a depth and an immediacy that belies the distance that separated them. Spencer in his turn was involved in a detailed correspondence of his own with his mentors in England, Tylor and Frazer, and in Melbourne was able to discuss theoretical ideas with the two pioneers of Australian anthropology A.W. Howitt and Lorimer Fison (see Mulvaney and Calaby 1985:198; Mulvaney 1987). Frazer in particular encouraged Spencer and Gillen to publish their work and used it himself in support of the theories he was putting forward about the origins of totemism. The debates that were sparked in Europe sent questions back to Spencer in Melbourne that Spencer in turn took with him into the field. In such ways ideas developed in

Figure 72.
QUEENSLAND –
CAPE YORK
Spear
Original Pitt Rivers
Collection
1884.19.8

Figure 73.
N. TERRITORY –
PORT DARWIN
Spear
Collected by
Captain Halpin
Transferred from
University Museum
1887.1.242

Figure 74. S. AUSTRALIA
Shield
Collected by G. H. Cox,
Victoria, 1864
1886.1.1602

Figure 75. N. TERRITORY
Shield
Collected by Rev. T. H. T. Hopkins
Transferred from
University Museum
1890.47.6

Figure 76. S. AUSTRALIA –
NEAR ADELAIDE –
'HIGHERCOMBE'
Shield
Collected by Mr. T. Giles c.1859
Donated by Major W. F. Anstey
1929.39.6

Figure 77. W. AUSTRALIA –
NULLAGINE
Shield
Collected by and purchased from
E. Clement
1898.75.14

Figure 78. W. AUSTRALIA
Shield
Collected by Edwin Hall
before 1910
Donated by T. Naish
1965.11.30

Figure 79. W. AUSTRALIA –
NULLAGINE
Shield
Collected by and purchased from
E. Clement
1898.75.15

Europe and America became part of Gillen's discourse with the Arrente, even though Spencer overtly tried to avoid prejudicing Gillen with theory (cf. Mulvaney and Calaby 1985:170).

'If [your conclusions] are well founded, it seems that the root of the whole system of exogamy is an aversion to marriages between brothers and sisters (as Morgan supposed). Now, what is the savage reason for that aversion? Put Gillen on the track of this. I conjecture it is some superstition we have not yet fathomed.'

Letter from Frazer to Spencer, 6.2.1899

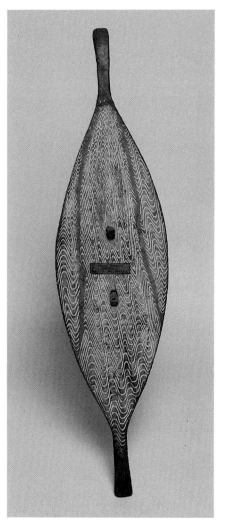

Figure 80. VICTORIA – MURRAY RIVER?
Shield
Original Pitt Rivers Collection
1884.30.14

58

'I have worked out the class system of the Chilchica very carefully and am sending you the result with other material ... Do please let me have a list of questions by each mail. I must have the guidance of your scientifically trained mind to work by or I shall accomplish very little ... If you will continue to direct my enquiries I am sure we will be able to collect a mass of valuable information.'

Letter from Gillen to Spencer, 7.11.1895

Perhaps it is not surprising considering Spencer's intellectual heritage that although his enterprise was able to reveal the great richness of Central Australian culture it was a richness that to the end of his life Spencer denied. Spencer had set out for Australia with the evolutionary models of Tylor and Pitt Rivers firmly in mind and in his subsequent work he used Frazer as his main inspiration as well as his literary agent and proof-reader. Spencer almost literally sought facts to prove or defend Frazer's theory. The urgency with which he took to the task was motivated by his desire to record a stone age society before it was too late, in order to gain insight into the origins of human culture.

Building on the work of Howitt, Spencer was able to reveal the complex structure of Central Australia kinship systems, but tended to place them as an early stage of human social organisation. In his descriptions of Aboriginal ceremonies he was the first to portray the vividness of the religious action, the complexity of the songs and dances and the depths of the emotion felt, yet at the same time he was concerned to deny that this was religion. According to Frazer's theories Aborigines were at a stage of cultural development that preceded religion.

Spencer to Frazer, 23.7.1902:

'I feel more than ever convinced that judging from our Australian tribe as a fair example of savages, your theory of magic, preceding religion is the true one.'

Frazer to Spencer, 14.7.1902:

'It is particularly gratifying to me to find that our theory of Australian totemism has been so strongly confirmed by the new evidence, and further that ... the Central tribes are the most primitive of all.'

However there is much evidence, as Mulvaney has argued, (Mulvaney and Calaby 1985:390), that Spencer's writings far from denying Aboriginal religion provided key insights into it and paved the way for its recognition. Mulvaney argues that Spencer got to the heart of Aboriginal religion by showing the relationship between people, their land and the Ancestral Past or Dreamtime. Aboriginal religion is centred on the spiritual continuity that exists between each succeeding generation and founding Ancestors who created the form of the landscape through their actions, and established the social and moral order of the universe. Paintings and engravings on objects are signs of the spiritual connection between the present and the creative acts of the past, a sign of the continuity of religious practice. Paintings were also integral to people's social identity and often took the form of abstract maps of the landscape in which they lived, representing its totemic or mythical dimension. Spencer recognised all of this but in the end had to deny his insight: 'to emphasize his social and philosophical ambience, Spencer reminded readers – that no matter how elaborate were the rituals described "it must be remembered that these ceremonies are performed by naked howling savages"' (Mulvaney and Calaby 1985:214).

Spencer fortunately had no final control over how his and Gillen's book would be read by others and from the beginning some of his contemporaries read the *Native Tribes of Central Australia* as a testament to Aboriginal religion and a defence of Aboriginal society. Spencer's field methods and his analysis of data enabled him to show much of the internal logic of Aboriginal society. In his writings it ceased to be a bundle of isolated culture traits and become a functioning system in its own right, and because of this it

became much harder to pigeon-hole Aboriginal society as some incoherent survival from an earlier stage. A key response in this respect was that of Constable Cowle the police officer in charge of Illaminta some 100 miles South of Alice Springs and a long term helper of Spencer and Gillen. On the publication of the *Native Tribes of Central Australia* he wrote to Spencer of his concern at the 'growth of the new cult of "Spencer and Gillenism" or the natives as human beings ... Anyone reading about the Arunta blacks might easily be led to believe that they only wanted wings or haloes' (cited from Mulvaney and Calaby 1985:130). In Europe Spencer and Gillen's writings were seized upon by armchair theorists of a very different persuasion to Frazer and Tylor and the absurd attempt to deny Aborigines religion by the evolutionary label 'magic' was to last very little longer. The vividness of their data and the detail of their accounts subtly changed the nature of the discourse away from Aborigines as exemplars of early stages of human evolution to understanding Aboriginal religion in its own right. This shift from an evolutionary paradigm to one in which cultures were understood first in their own terms, represented a shift from theories of racial superiority to seeing again the essential unity and equality of mankind.

'Had no idea that native life amongst the blacks would have been so full of rites and ceremonies. I suppose they are almost lowest of all men, and yet they have shown themselves, or rather you have shown them to have so much in common with the rest of mankind.'
Cecil Wilson, Bishop of Melanesia to Spencer, 8.19.1899.

Reading between the lines of Spencer and Gillen's books and reading Gillen's letters one cannot help feeling that the direction of movement towards a positive image of Aboriginal society was one with which they were in sympathy. In their advocacy of Aboriginal rights, their concern for Aboriginal welfare and their attitude to Aboriginal culture Spencer and

Gillen were both well ahead of their time. They probably went as far as they could without stepping outside the society in which they lived, and as gregarious and in many respects conventional figures of their times such a step would have been unlikely. Yet it is clear that Gillen in particular identified emotionally with the Aborigines of Central Australia far more than he was ever able to admit. Although officially he had remained so long in Central Australia in the interests of science, so that he could keep the information flowing to Europe, his sentiments on leaving employment in the Centre for the last time are significant: 'I shall feel parting with the blacks much more than with the whites' (Letter from Gillen to Spencer, 15.4.1899).

★   ★   ★

'Works such as yours . . ., recording a phase of human history which before long will have passed away, will have a permanent value so long as men exist on earth and take an interest in their own past. Books like mine, merely speculative, will be superseded sooner or later (the sooner the better for the sake of truth) by better inductions based on fuller knowledge; books like yours, containing records of observation, can never be superseded.'

Letter from Frazer to Spencer, 13.7.1898

Spencer and Gillen's books changed the direction of anthropology by setting a new standard in the recording of ethnographic facts. However, the implicit message of the equality of Aboriginal society took a much longer time to be absorbed. Spencer to the end of his life believed that Aborigines were a dying race and after the initial explosion of interest at the turn of the century Aborigines faded again in the European imagination. As they faded less interest was taken in their art and material culture. In Australia itself Aborigines became invisible to the majority of white Australians who had no contact with them in their daily lives and who saw them as part of Australia's past. Indeed to the vast majority of Australians Aborigines were of little political

significance between the time of the First World War and the late 1950s, when through their own actions they began to make their voice heard again.

In anthropology over the same period there was a shift away from material culture towards social facts. It was in writing not in photographs or through material objects that the cultural relativist message of modern anthropology was first put across and that the complex nature of Aboriginal society was demonstrated. The works of anthropologists such as Warner, Stanner and Elkin set about establishing the equality of Aboriginal society through intellectual debate and the phrase 'a society with simple technology but complex kinship systems and religion' became almost an anti-evolutionist cliché. This uncritical acceptance of the simplicity of their material culture may have been one factor that slowed down the collecting process: enough was felt to be known about it already. Indeed once Henry Balfour, the first curator of the Pitt Rivers Museum had acquired in 1900 the Hardy collection, one of the largest private collections of Aboriginal objects with a wide geographical coverage, he may have thought his task largely completed. A representative collection of Australian objects existed and there was after all room for only a certain number of boomerangs. Another important factor was that no aesthetic appreciation of Aboriginal material culture and art had developed by the turn of the century. The same social evolutionist perspective that denied religion to the Aborigines, denied them the possibility of art. Moreover much of the beauty of Aboriginal culture was imminent in ritual action and expressed in a transient form in the great but impermanent ceremonial constructions that the performance entailed.

It is only in recent years that the insights into the complexity of Aboriginal culture have been transferred back to their material culture and there has been some reintegration in the museum context of the material and non-material expressions of Aboriginal values. In particular since the 1960s Aboriginal art, the designs on objects, paintings on grave posts and human bodies, sculptures formed in sand, have begun to be understood as central to the transmission of the Dreamtime, as ways of encoding messages from the Ancestral Past about relationships between people and land (see e.g., Munn 1973, Ucko 1977). And as the value of art to Aboriginal society has begun to be appreciated so too has the art itself. Aboriginal art is characterised by its enormous variety, ranging from the intricate engraved designs of the Southeast, through the predominently geometric traditions of the Centre and the bold abstract form of the Queensland rainforest to the complex figurative traditions of Western Arnhem Land. Much of the art such as the sand sculptures and body paintings is impermanent; other forms are more durable, such as the massive iron wood grave posts, bark baskets and elaborately carved spears associated with the Pukamani ceremony of the Tiwi of Melville and Bathurst Island. There is also an increased appreciation of the elegant simplicity and fine craftsmanship of some of the everyday material culture of the Aborigines: the balanced form of the spear throwers from Cape York and the beautifully structured bicornual baskets from the same region, the functional elegance of some of the boomerangs from the Southeast, and the fine textured finish of the richly ochred and fluted objects that come from Central Australia.

Central Australia has changed since the days of Spencer and Gillen. Alice Springs has become a thriving Australian town. But the Aborigines of Central Australia are still there and continue to assert their spiritual continuity with the land. Many adjustments have been made to European colonisation, but the same songs Spencer recorded on his wax cylinders nearly 100 years ago are still being sung today. The Aborigines of Central Australia have been extraordinarily resilient in maintaining their culture and their autonomy in the face of the invasion of their land. The most recent acquisitions by the Pitt Rivers Museum include paintings on canvas from Central Australia – paintings of subjects that Spencer would have found familiar. Indeed they are remarkably similar in form to some of those recorded by Spencer as ground drawings used in rituals that he watched all those years ago. The difference in this case is that Aborigines have learnt to broadcast their culture themselves albeit to an audience that, partly as a result of Spencer and his successors, is more sensitive to its message.

REFERENCES

Chapman, W.R. 1985. Arranging Ethnology: A.H.L.F. Pitt Rivers and the Typological Tradition. In George W. Stocking, Jr. (ed) *Ojects and Others: Essays on Museums and Material Culture*. Madison: University of Wisconsin Press.

Lane Fox, A.H. (Pitt Rivers). 1874. *Catalogue of the Anthropological Collections*. London: Her Majesty's Stationery Office.

Munn, N. 1973. *Walbiri Iconography*. Ithaca: Cornell University Press.

Mulvaney, D.J. and J.H. Calaby. 1985. *So Much That is New*. Melbourne: Melbourne University Press.

Mulvaney, D.J. 1987. Patron and Client: the Web of Intellectual Kinship in Australian Anthropology. In W. Reingold and M. Rothenburg (eds) *Scientific Colonialism, a Cross-cultural Comparison*. Washington: Smithsonian Institution Press.

Spencer, W.B.S. and F.J. Gillen. 1899. *Native Tribes of Central Australia*. London: Macmillan.

Ucko, P.J. (ed) 1977. *Form in Indigenous Art*. London: Duckworth.

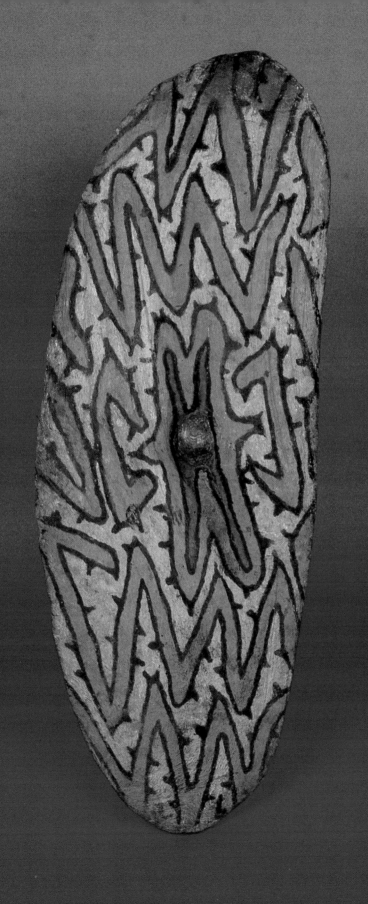

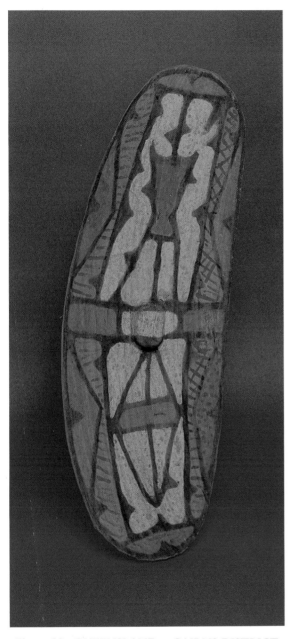

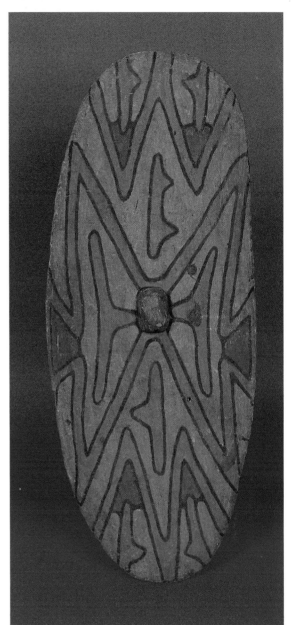

Figure 82. QUEENSLAND – CAIRNS DISTRICT
Shield
Donated by Rev. E. A. Dawson
1919.55.1

Figure 83. N. QUEENSLAND
Shield
Hardy Collection: probably collected by H. Stockdale
Donated by R. F. Wilkins
1900.55.164

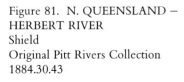

Figure 81. N. QUEENSLAND –
HERBERT RIVER
Shield
Original Pitt Rivers Collection
1884.30.43

Figure 84. QUEENSLAND
Shield
Hardy Collection: probably collected
by H. Stockdale
Donated by R. F. Wilkins
1900.55.165

Figure 85 above. QUEENSLAND – MORETON
BAY
Basket
Original Pitt Rivers Collection
1884.44.9

Figure 86 above right. S. QUEENSLAND –
WARREGO RIVER
Basket
Original Pitt Rivers Collection
1884.44.4

Figure 87 right. S. AUSTRALIA
Basket
Original Pitt Rivers Collection
1884.44.13

Figure 88 left.
QUEENSLAND
Basket
Donated by Dr. Turner,
Bishop of Grafton &
Armidale
1893.38.24

Figure 89 below.
S. AUSTRALIA –
COOPER'S CREEK –
INNAMINKA
Bag containing the narcotic
pituri
Donated by
Dr. E. C. Stirling
1897.8.1

Figure 90. N. TERRITORY – E. ALLIGATOR
RIVER – MERKINNALAL CREEK
Basket
Hardy Collection: collected by H. Stockdale
Donated by R. F. Wilkins
1900.55.218

Figure 91. N. TERRITORY – E. ALLIGATOR
RIVER – MERKINNALAL CREEK
Basket
Hardy Collection: probably collected by H. Stockdale
Donated by R. F. Wilkins
1900.55.221

Figure 92. N. TERRITORY – E. ALLIGATOR
RIVER – MERKINNALAL CREEK
Basket
Hardy Collection: probably collected by H. Stockdale
Donated by R. F. Wilkins

Figure 93. N. TERRITORY – E. ALLIGATOR
RIVER – MERKINNALAL CREEK
Basket
Hardy Collection: probably collected by H. Stockdale
Donated by R. F. Wilkins

Figure 95 top above. N. TERRITORY TABLELAND
NEAR ROPER RIVER
Brow ornament of painted stringwork with crocodile
teeth, and *abrus precatorius* seeds set in gum
Hardy Collection: probably collected by H. Stockdale
Donated by R. F. Wilkins
1900.55.258

Figure 96 above. N. TERRITORY – GULF OF
CARPENTARIA – ROPER RIVER DISTRICT –
?MARA TRIBE
Brow-band of stringwork, painted with animal figures
Collected by and purchased from A. H. Coltart
1935.71.5

Figure 94 right. N. TERRITORY
Dilly-bag
Hardy Collection: probably collected by H. Stockdale
Donated by R. F. Wilkins
1900.55.207

Figure 99. TASMANIA
Three necklets of iridescent shells
Outer specimens collected by Charles Smith c.1900-1910
Purchased from his executors
1928.87.332-333
Inner Specimen from Burchell Collection
Transferred from Ashmolean Museum
1886.1.1577

Figure 97 left. W. AUSTRALIA –
KIMBERLEY DISTRICT – BROOME
Man's pubic ornament of carved pearl shell
hung from belt of hair
Collected by and purchased from E. Clement
1898.75.70

Figure 98 below. N. TERRITORY –
MELVILLE ISLAND
Pendant of beeswax covered with *arbrus precatorius* seeds
Collected and donated by H. K. Fry
1917.6.33

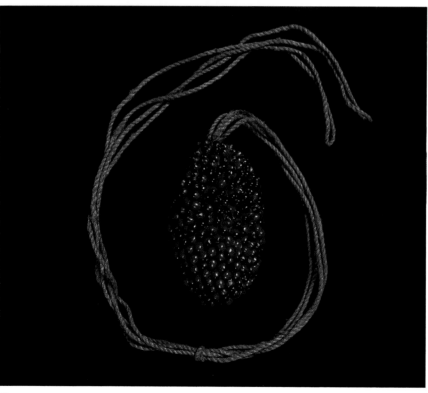

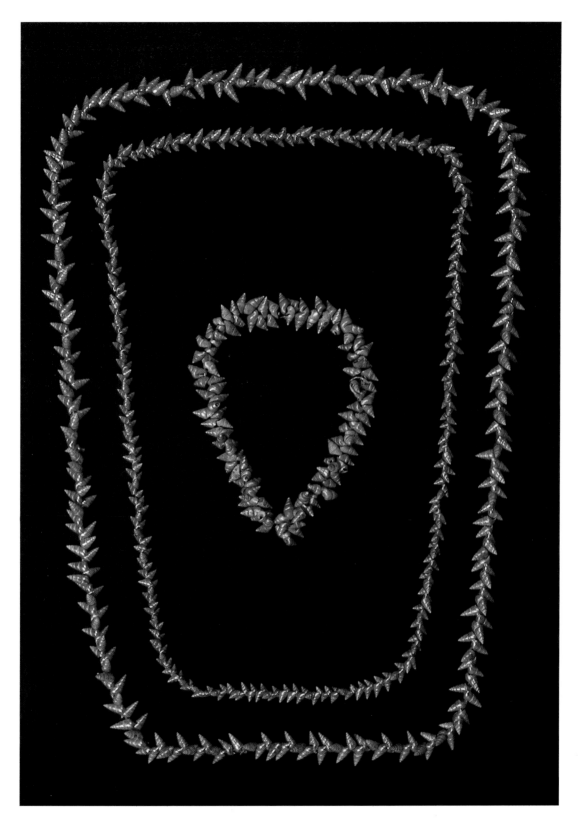

71

Figure 100 left.
N. TERRITORY –
WARAMANGA TRIBE
Two stone knives with
painted wood handles
Upper specimen from
Hardy Collection:
collected by H. Stockdale
Donated by R. F. Wilkins
1900.55.182
Lower specimen
collected by the
Spencer-Gillen
expedition 1901-2
Donated by
W. Baldwin Spencer
1903.39.40.1

Figure 101 below.
N. TERRITORY –
N. OF MACDONNELL
RANGES
Glass surgical knife with
sheath of paper-bark
Hardy Collection:
collected by
H. Stockdale
Donated by R. F. Wilkins
1900.55.225.1-2

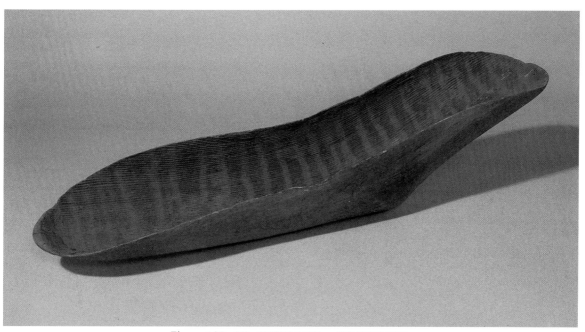

Figure 102. W. AUSTRALIA – KIMBERLEY
Pitchi used as a baby-carrier and food bowl
Collected and donated by W. Saville Kent
1896.50.4

Figure 103. TASMANIA
Model raft of bark
Collected by Sir John & Lady Franklin 1843
Donated by Eton College Museum
1893.50.13

Figure 104 left.
N. TERRITORY –
W. ARNHEM LAND –
OENKPELLI –
KUNWINJKU
Bark painting, probably
by the artist Yirawala.
It depicts the Rainbow
Serpent Ngalyod giving
birth to Aboriginal
people.
Bequeathed by
Dr. K. P. Oakley
1982.12.1

Figure 105 opposite.
N. TERRITORY –
ARNHEM LAND –
GROOT EYLANDT –
ANGURUGU MISSION
Bark painting by an artist
known as Kneepad. It
depicts the legend of a
woman (bottom of
painting) not yet of this
world who is wandering
around with No. 2 star
looking for a country to
settle in. They enlist the
help of the morning star,
who brings daylight.
Together they find the
earth (top of painting).
The morning star creates
the sun and man, giving
man a spear to hunt.
Purchased from
Miss Gale Hobbins
1967.38.1

Figure 106.
N. TERRITORY
Painting on canvas by the artist Pansy Nakamarra Stewart. It depicts women in the dreaming country of Wapurtali, digging for bush carrot or bush potato. The circles represent camp or digging sites, the semi-circles women, and the straight lines roots. Purchased from Warlukurlangu Artists Association
1987.26.1

Figure 107. N. TERRITORY
Painting on canvas by the artist Esther
Nungarrayi Fry, entitled *Kunajarraya Dreaming*. It
depicts a dreaming known as PuWitiPu in the
Kunajarrayi country. PuWitiPu is the name
given to ceremonial poles tied to the legs of
male dancers at the initiation of young men.
These poles are represented by wavy lines and
short straight strokes. The concentric circles
between the wavy lines are witchetty bushes
with witchetty grubs in their roots.
Purchased from Warlukurlangu Artists
Association
1987.26.2

7. "The Foundations of All Good and Noble Principles" Oxonians and the Australian Universities in the Nineteenth Century

by Richard Symonds

Oxford men went out to teach in the Australian Universities in the nineteenth century for a variety of reasons. Many decided to go because they were disqualified on marriage from holding College fellowships and were not content to become, or remain, country parsons or schoolmasters in England. Some were attracted by the generous salaries of the Australian professorships. Some went for their health, others because they felt cramped by the Church of England's hold on education in Oxford and the nation. With such reasons were often combined a sense of adventure and a desire to exercise a broader influence than they could expect to have at home. Besides those who went out intending to teach, there were men who had originally come out to farm, but failing, or finding the work too arduous or lonely, turned to education as the most obvious profession in which an Oxford degree had a market value.

When the earliest Australian University was established in Sydney in 1850, a Committee of Selection in London was asked by the Provost and Colonial Secretary to recommend as its first professors "men of high academical distinction, either from Oxford or Cambridge". The professors were also to be, in a phrase borrowed from Dr Thomas Arnold, "qualified to assist in laying the foundations of all good and noble principles" (Barff 1902:16).

Rev. John Woolley, who was appointed at the age of 36 as the first Principal and Professor of Classics, was a notable scholar, who had been obliged to resign his fellowship at University College, Oxford on marriage and had since been Headmaster of Hereford, Rossall and Norwich Schools, where he had introduced the educational methods of Dr Thomas Arnold.

Woolley's devotion to Oxford was unlimited,

and in his address at the inaugural ceremony of Sydney University he declared, with some historical licence:

"980 years have passed since our glorious King Alfred provided amidst the fens and forests of

Figure 108. Rev. John Woolley, First Principal, University of Sydney
W. M. Tweedie, 1865
(University of Sydney Collection)

78

Oxford a home for the poor and scattered scholars who were, in those rude and uncertain times, with toil and danger watching before the pale and glimmering light of knowledge. Did his imagination dare her flight beyond the limit of his island home, and picture in the remotest corners of the earth the children of his race, nurtured in his own institutions, bearing forth the spirit and forms which they loved into a yet wider solitude and a more inaccessible wilderness?"

As he looked into the future, he hoped that "the bays of Sydney harbour will mirror many a reverend chapel and pictured hall and solemn cloister like those that gem the Isis and the Cam; whose memory like some choice perfume revives the spirit fainting under the cares and business of life" (Woolley 1862:4ff).

Woolley was a close friend of A.P. Stanley, Arnold's biographer, who was Secretary of the first Commission on the Reform of Oxford University. When he arrived it had been envisaged that the new university would be modelled on that of London and have only an examining role, whilst the teaching would be done in the constituent colleges, to which the professors would be attached. Woolley however persuaded those responsible to adopt the Oxford reformed model, by which the professors taught in the university and the college students were obliged to attend their lectures. He further strengthened the position of the professors by enabling them to become members of the Senate, and emphasized the secular character of the university by eliminating the requirement that students must present a certificate of attainment in religious studies from their colleges before being allowed to graduate.

Whilst Woolley's influence on the constitution of Sydney University, upon which those of the other Australian universities were largely modelled, was of great importance, as Principal and Professor he was less successful in imposing his philosophy of the role of a university in a new colony.

He was an ardent Platonist, seeing the main purpose of university as the preparation through a liberal classical arts curriculum of a colonial governing class drawn from all ranks of society. The university must not be functional – "the soundest lawyers", he said in his inaugural speech, "come from schools in which law is never taught. The most accomplished physicians are nurtured where medicine is but a name" (Woolley 1862:13).

But between 1859 and 1865 the University produced only 50 graduates; the local secondary schools were unable to provide sufficient candidates with the knowledge of classics required for entry. Woolley's bold assertion that the purpose of the University was to offset materialism, and his opposition to vocational studies, offended many of Sydney's influential citizens. His belief that it was the duty of academics to take their knowledge outside the university led him to give public lectures on Aristotle which were misunderstood; the Anglican hierarchy protested to the University Senate, and he was accused of "instilling philosophical and political notions which might ripen into vulgar and rampant radicalism" (Gardner 1979:52). Even the Chancellor, Sir Charles Nicholson, wrote that "he has genius, learning and great amiability of character, and yet in some of his sayings evinces an entire absence of common sense" (Gardner 1979:52, and see MacMillan 1973).

Woolley died in 1866, an unhappy and disappointed man, in a shipwreck whilst returning from England where he had tried in vain to obtain another post.

He was succeeded as Professor of Classics by Rev. Charles Badham of Wadham College who was already 54 when he arrived. Badham, who had undertaken research in the Vatican, Germany, France and Holland, was regarded as one of the most eminent Greek scholars in Europe, but marriage prevented him from holding a fellowship at Oxford or Cambridge; and his open support of F.D. Maurice proved an obstacle to promotion in the Church. He became headmaster of a private school in Birmingham and applied for the Sydney post because he considered that it would allow him more time for scholarship. Generous, bluff and irascible, Sydney took him to its heart as a "character". Determined that the University should be opened to all classes, he spent his vacations travelling around the colony collecting money for bursaries. A professor, he said, must look upon his leisure as no longer his own and must be accessible to all who desire to consult him. In this spirit he made an offer through the local press to receive and criticize without payment translation exercises in Greek, Latin, French and German from clerks, teachers, mechanics and others from anywhere in the colony.

No one who heard him, wrote the editor of his speeches, "will ever forget the trembling voice and faltering accents with which he read Plato's story of the last hours of Socrates nor the fiery passion with which he held forth the invective of Demosthenes or the last speech of Dido ... He also set himself to preserve among us propriety in the pronunciation of English, and occasionally brought a blush to the cheek of his scholars by imitating their barbarous pronunciation, especially of the letter 'i' and diphthong 'ow'" (Badham 1890:xxxii). Nobody else perhaps would have dared to tell the elite of Sydney in a university commemoration address, that "Dingo English" was as bad as "Dog Latin" (Badham 1890:40). He was blunt and unsparing in his criticisms. He attacked the "hierarchy of ignorance and incapacity in all our government offices, and the dismal burlesque of examination for the Civil Service." He told businessmen that "if you wish that the professions should not degenerate into trades, if you wish to have sermons that you can listen to without disgust, physic that you can swallow with some hope of amendment, law to which you can have recourse with some chance of being righted ... make your sons scholars and let your daughters help them in the endeavour" (Badham 1890:59).

He was realistic enough however to persuade the University to relieve arts students from the burden of compulsory Greek. He died in harness at the age of 70, and his coffin was carried to the

Figure 109. Rev. Charles Badham, Professor of Classics
G. Anivitti, 1875
(University of Sydney Collection)

grave by men from many walks of life who had been not only his formal but his informal pupils.

Between Badham's death and the arrival of his successor a year later the duties of Professor of Classics were carried out with remarkable versatility by W.J. Stephen, Professor of Natural History and graduate of The Queen's College, Oxford.

The next Professor of Classics, Walter Scott, who held the chair from 1884 to 1900, had been an undergraduate at Balliol, where he won the Ireland, Craven and Derby Scholarships, and a Fellow of Merton. He was a notable scholar and something of a recluse, though he played a leading part in the establishment of a women's

80

college in the University and in organizing extension work. He eventually returned to England on grounds of bad health (see Serle 1949:312).

When a separate chair in history was established, Scott asked A.L. Smith, Balliol's Modern History tutor, to recommend a candidate. This was G. Arnold Wood who was 26 when he arrived in Sydney in 1891 to hold the chair for nearly 40 years. He came from a nonconformist family, and after taking a first in Modern History read Theology, hoping to become a university teacher "engaged in a cure of souls"; but his studies caused him to become an agnostic.

He brought with him from Balliol a high sense of duty. "The purpose of history", he declared in his inaugural lecture, "is to enable the student in his turn to make history ... History should be studied primarily as the history of the human spirit in its noblest manifestations" (Crawford 1975:132). He expressed his contempt for those students of history "who take their first classes, are elected to fellowships and leave the foolish world outside the Common Room to solve the problems of life ... unhelped and unguided" (Crawford 1975:153).

A professor who proclaimed that the duty of the historian was to find a lesson for the present in the study of the past was unlikely to avoid controversy. Although professing to be an Imperialist, Wood attacked the Boer War as unjust, and was rebuked by the Senate, which resolved that his articles and public speeches were unworthy of a Professor of History. Throughout his career he wrote articles for the Manchester Guardian, championing Irish Home Rule and opposing Imperial Federation. He turned his moral analysis enthusiastically to Australian history, and, with the excusable hyperbole of the experienced lecturer, described the English politicians, lawyers and bishops of 100 years earlier as atrocious criminals, whose innocent victims were sent out as convicts and founded Australian democracy. He was a brilliant teacher and writer of narrative history, many of whose students were to hold appointments in Australian and other universities in the next generation (Farrell et al. 1952:63).

From 1855 until 1880 the Registrar of Sydney University was Hugh Kennedy who was also Assistant Professor of Classics. He had studied at Balliol, but there is some doubt as to whether he took the B.A. degree which he later claimed. He died in the hospital for the insane, his mental illness having probably been brought about by unsuccessful land speculations (see Australian Dictionary of Biography Vol. 3:15).

That Sydney University's student enrolment eventually increased was in no small measure due to A.B. Weigall who was Headmaster of Sydney Grammar School from 1866 to 1912. There were 53 pupils in the school when he arrived and 696 when he died. A Brasenose man, he had been inspired by the lectures of T.H. Green to undertake a career of public service; but he injured his health by overworking for his degree and was sent on a sea voyage to recover. In the course of this he heard that the family solicitor had embezzled the estate, and so took a teaching post in Australia to support his sisters. He brought to Sydney Grammar School two other Oxford men as assistant masters. Together they not only educated boys who met the University's entrance requirements, but introduced most of the institutions of the English public schools, including competitive football and cricket, an annual athletics meeting, prefects, school magazine and a debating society (see McCallum 1913; Turney 1969:115).

When the University of Melbourne was founded in 1852, it was decided that its first professors should not be in Holy Orders, though they should have "such habits and manners as to stamp on their future pupils the character of loyal well bred Englishmen" (Scott 1936:21–22). The exclusion of clergymen caused a rather different type of Oxford man to come to Melbourne than those who had helped to establish Sydney University. M.H. Irving, a graduate of Balliol, who was appointed as Professor of Classics in 1856, was the son of the founder of the Irvingite religious sect and as a member of it was ineligible for an Oxford college fellowship. Aged only 25, he immediately took charge of laying out the University grounds and founded a boat club in which he stroked the first boat. He succeeded in persuading the University to examine for degrees students who were unable to attend its courses; he failed to persuade it however to abolish compulsory Greek in the arts degree course. Even his energetic nature eventually rebelled against having to give 450 lectures a year in Greek, Latin, English and Logic. He resigned to accept a more lucrative post as Headmaster of Wesley College, from which he continued however to exercise a considerable influence in the University Council, continually pressing for a reform of the curriculum in favour of the natural sciences (see Blainey 1957:41).

Irving's close friend and ally on the University Council was C.H. Pearson, a Fellow of Oriel, who had originally come out for health reasons as a farmer. Pearson was briefly a lecturer in Modern History in the University, but it made little effort to retain the services of the man who was to become the outstanding intellectual of the Australian colonies in the nineteenth century. Pearson was allowed no say in the curriculum and textbooks, and was required to reapply for his post at the end of the year. Perhaps his main contribution was to found a Debating Society in the city along the lines of the Oxford Union, of which he had been President, for present and former students of the University; this became a nursery of future leaders in Australian politics and society. He was offered the new Chair of Modern History at Adelaide, but, having a strong interest in female education, he accepted instead the headmastership of the Melbourne Presbyterian Ladies College, where the income from salary and fees considerably exceeded the stipend of a university professor. Compelled to resign from this post for expressing radical views on the land question, which shocked the parents, he entered the Legislative Assembly, where he promptly introduced a bill which admitted women students to the University. Later, as a

Commissioner and Minister of Education, he did much to bring about expansion of the teaching of science and engineering in the University. He was a hundred years ahead of his time however in proposing the abolition of fees for its lectures and examinations (see Blainey 1957:54–63; Tregenza 1968).

Irving was succeeded as Professor of Classics in 1872 by H.A. Strong, a graduate of Corpus, aged 24, who managed to continue while at Melbourne to publish editions and translations of Latin authors, but after 11 years returned to England to a chair in the new University of Liverpool. Like Irving, he participated keenly in athletics. He advocated the teaching of modern languages in the University; outside it he was a popular lecturer on literary subjects and campaigned successfully for the opening of public libraries and museums on Sundays. His son became Professor of English at Adelaide (see Blainey 1957:108; Australian Dictionary of Biography Vol. 6:209).

In 1884 E.E. Morris, a graduate of Lincoln College, was appointed to the new Chair of English, French and German Languages, in which he had to lecture single handed. He had come out originally as Headmaster of Melbourne Grammar School, where he changed the school colours to Oxford Blue. Known as the "Philanthropic Professor", he was the founding President of the Charity Organization Society and among his many causes were the higher education of women, church unity, and academic freedom. The last of these causes needed champions; professors were not allowed in early years to lecture outside the Univeristy without permission of the Council. Morris, when he sought permission to lecture on Tennyson's *Idylls of the King*, was warned not to dabble in politics or religion, and Baldwin Spencer received a similar admonition when he proposed to lecture on the Aborigines at Geelong College (see Australian Dictionary of Biography Vol. 5:293; Scott 1936:441–445). The *Oxford Magazine* in 1891 published a letter from a former Melbourne professor, Edward Jenks, warning Oxford men not to apply for posts in a university controlled by laymen who would not tolerate academic freedom (see *Oxford Magazine* Vol. 9, 1891:232).

The Oxford man who made perhaps the greatest impact on Melbourne in the late 19th and early 20th centuries was not a classicist but its first Professor of Biology, Baldwin Spencer.

Spencer was a graduate of Exeter College, a Fellow of Lincoln, and a member of the small but distinguished group of ardent Darwinists who were pupils of the zoologist H.V. Moseley. He had helped Moseley and E.B. Tylor, the first Reader in Anthropology, to set up the Pitt Rivers Museum in Oxford.

Figure 110. Sir Baldwin Spencer
W. B. McInnes, 1924
(Exeter College, Oxford)

On his appointment to the Melbourne chair at the age of 26 he immediately married. He hustled the University into providing a much larger appropriation than had been envisaged for staff and laboratories; but for the first two years Spencer and his wife wistfully went down to watch every departing steamer for England. Eventually he settled down to make a remarkably broad contribution to the University, to Victoria and indeed to Australia.

In addition to setting up his department, he was a frequent and brilliant popular lecturer. He was a member of the Horn expedition which explored Central Australia, and wrote its report. Later he organized his own travels into the interior. Drawn more and more into anthropology, learning Aboriginal languages and winning their confidence, he believed that among them could be found the key to the interpretation of the social and religious evolution of mankind. His findings were enthusiastically incorporated by Sir James Frazer into *The Golden Bough*, and the unique knowledge revealed in his books on Central and Northern Australia caused the Australian Government to appoint him for a year as Chief Protector of the aborigines in the Northern Territory.

Apart from his work as a biologist and anthropologist, Spencer was for many years Chairman of the University's Professorial Board, Director of the National Museum of Victoria, and an influential patron of Australian art. He was knighted in 1916; on his retirement, at which time all the staff of his department were women, he offered to remain as honorary Reader in Anthropology, in which the University had no established post. His offer was ignored and he returned to England, from where he set out on one last anthropological journey to Tierra del Fuego, in whose harsh climate he met his death (see Mulvaney and Calaby 1985; Marrett and Penniman 1931).

In Melbourne University each of the colleges was founded by a religious denomination, and their heads exercised considerable influence on the Council of the "Godless" University. Alexander Leeper, an Irish graduate of St John's College, Oxford, became Warden of the Church of England Trinity College in 1876 at the age of 27 and held the post for 42 years. He had first come out to Australia to a temporary post as a private tutor and had fallen in love with the sister of one of his pupils. He returned a second time as a master at Melbourne College to pursue his courtship and because of incipient TB. At Trinity he introduced a tutorial system which enabled the College's students to win most of the University prizes and scholarships. He saw the duty of the College as not only to teach scholarship but citizenship, inspired by residential tutors. The strictness of his regime brought about a student rebellion and a public investigation by the Church authorities, but he survived the crisis, always seeking opportunities to exercise his four "Passionate Loyalties", to the Church, the Classics, the Act of Union (between Britain and Ireland) and the British Empire. Somewhat unusually he combined these with support for feminism, establishing a women's hostel in the College and advocating the ordination of women in the Church of England (see Australian Dictionary of Biography Vol. 10:54).

Adelaide University was founded in 1874, largely through the efforts of the Anglican Bishop Augustus Short, who had been Gladstone's tutor at Christ Church, Oxford. Although he was a High Churchman, Short had been long enough in South Australia, "The paradise of dissent", to realize that an Oxford model would be unacceptable, and instead Adelaide adopted the Scottish non-residential pattern. Short however in his address as Vice Chancellor at the inaugural ceremony described the purpose of universities in terms which contemporary Oxford would have heartily approved, as

"Directing the studies and forming the character of the governing classes of every Christian country; they help to elevate the middle class to higher civilisation, the result of a more intellectual education. They afford quiet retreats for students of Literature and the theoretical parts of

Figure 111. Professor George Henderson, University of Adelaide. (Barr Smith Library)

Science and Philosophy. Finally they award Literary and Scientific honours" (Duncan and Leonard 1973:8; see also Whitington 1887).

Adelaide recruited its early Professors of Classics from Cambridge, but of its first eight Professors of History, between 1900 and 1970, seven were Oxford men. The first of these was G.C. Henderson, the son of a New South Wales coal miner: he was a student of Arnold Wood at Sydney and then went on a scholarship to Wood's old college, Balliol; thus doubly exposed to Balliol idealism, he came to Adelaide as Professor of English as well as of History. He taught that poetry had a message for democracy and that love of nature should be cultivated as an antidote against the scramble to outdo one's fellows in material possessions. His lectures were so popular that they had to be transferred from the University to the Town Hall; and the Governor and Premier of South Australia would send telegrams of apology if unable to attend. He did much to encourage the interest of Australian universities in the study of Australian history and in opening up archives for the purpose. The obverse side to his charismatic character was deep periodic depression, and he died by his own hand twenty years after his early retirement from the Chair (see Casson 1964:22 and *passim*; Symonds 1986:309–310).

In the next century two Adelaide graduates were to contribute much to Oxford. It was on Henderson's advice that Hugh Cairns went to Balliol, where he married the youngest of the seven daughters of A.L. Smith, the Master, and so became brother-in-law to a number of important members of the English Establishment. He was to be instrumental in bringing Lord Nuffield's great benefactions to Oxford medicine and became the first Professor of Surgery under them. His even more famous Adelaide contemporary, Howard Florey, the discoverer of penicillin, was Professor of Pathology and Provost of The Queen's College.

The first Oxford women's colleges opened in 1879, and before 1914 only 11 Oxford women can be seen from the college registers to have worked in Australia and New Zealand, mostly as teachers. Several daughters of Oxford men in the Australian universities however had important careers in education. The two daughters of Irving were successively Headmistress of Lauriston Girls School. Edith Badham, who studied all the subjects in the arts course at Sydney University, became so proficient that she helped her father to correct examination papers. Later she was the first Principal of the Sydney Church of England Girls Grammar School, where she insisted that it was possible for a girl to learn Latin or Greek "without at all desiring to step out of her proper and subordinate place in the scheme of creation" (Australian Dictionary of Biography Vol. 7:130).

Even after Australia had its own universities, Australians came to Oxford to study, sometimes after taking degrees at home. In 1886 between 25 to 30 Australians were studying in Oxford (see *Oxford Magazine* Vol. 4, 1886). Among those at Balliol in the 1880s were the three sons of Sir J.F. Fairfax, proprietor of the Sydney Morning Herald. The family were to continue coming to Balliol in the next two generations. Sir Ernest Barker recollected the Australians in the 1890s, "with the sunshine in their veins, they bubbled with ready fun; they blew into the antiquity of Oxford, with the challenge of their own and their country's youth" (Barker 1953:323). G.V. Portus, who came up in 1907 and returned to teach at Adelaide, recorded the intellectual excitement of tutorials and the broad tolerance of all opinions; he also remembered the apparent aloofness of English undergraduates, against which the reaction of Australians was bumptious. It took them some time, he said, to admit that the British Empire existed because of, and not in spite of, Britain (see Portus 1983:89).

By the end of the century brilliant Australians were beginning to remain and teach in Oxford. Gilbert Murray became a Fellow of New College in 1883 and Professor of Greek in 1908, and the philosopher Samuel Alexander became a Fellow of Lincoln in 1882. After the Rhodes Scholars started to come to Oxford at the beginning of the 20th century, the contribution of Australians to

Oxford became as important as that of British Oxonians in Australia.

Many of the issues with which the Oxford men were concerned in the Australian universities in the nineteenth century were simultaneously being debated in Oxford itself, where Jowett and his friends sought to free the University from the predominance of ecclesiasticism and restore it to the nation. On these questions – admission of women, abolition of compulsory Greek, introduction and expansion of modern subjects, and the extension of the University's reach to the wider community – the Oxonians in Australia were almost always on the side of the reformers, and the reforms in Australia came earlier than those in Oxford.

To survive, so far from home, and in an environment which often seemed distressingly uncultured, three qualities in particular were needed. Each of these can be illustrated among the many letters which over a period of 50 years L.R. Phelps, Fellow and eventually Provost of Oriel College, received from his former pupils working in Australia and all over the Empire, although these happen to have been written a little later than our period.

The sense of duty required was expressed in a letter in 1932 from a lecturer in economics at the University of Tasmania, who was also a consultant to the Australian Government, – "to keep a turbulent, headstrong and inexperienced people within the bounds of economic sense," he confided, "is an uninspiring task, and one sees little result, but it is a kind of pioneering" (J.R. Brigden to Phelps, Nov. 13, 1932. In L.R. Phelps MSS).

The optimism needed appears in a letter from a teacher of theology and philosophy in Victoria in 1915: "I cannot say that theology is very advanced, or philosophy, or any form of culture, but all these will come. There will be a glorious civilization in Australia, I feel inspired to predict" (F. Spencer to Phelps, Jan. 19, 1915. In L.R. Phelps MSS).

But the essential quality was sympathy, to feel, as a Master at Geelong Grammar School rather naively told Phelps in 1930, that "the Australians are so much nicer than people at home will ever admit" (J.R. Darling to Phelps, June 7, 1930. In L.R. Phelps MSS).

REFERENCES

Australian Dictionary of Biography.

Badham, C. 1890. *Speeches and Lectures Delivered in Australia.* Sydney.

Barff, H.E. 1902. *Short Historical Account of the University of Sydney.* Sydney.

Barker, E. 1953. *Age and Youth.* London.

Blainey, G. 1957. *Centenary History of the University of Melbourne.* Melbourne.

Casson, M.R. 1964. G.C. Henderson. *South Australia* Vol. III.

Crawford, R.M. 1975. *A Bit of a Rebel: The Life of G.A. Wood.* Sydney.

Duncan, W.A.C. and R.A. Leonard. 1973. *The University of Adelaide.* Adelaide.

Farrell, R.B. *et al.* 1952. *100 Years of the Faculty of Arts.* Sydney.

Gardner, W.J. 1979. *Colonial Cap & Gown.* Canterbury (N.Z.)

McCullum, M.W. 1913. *A.B. Weigall.* Sydney.

Macmillan, D.S. 1963. The University of Sydney 1850–1870, in *The Australian University.* Vol.1, pp.26–59.

Marett, R.R. and T.K. Penniman. 1931. *Spencer's Last Journey.* Oxford.

Mulvaney, D.J. and J.H. Calaby. 1985. *So Much That is New: Baldwin Spencer, 1860–1929.* Melbourne.

Oxford Magazine Vol.4, 1886.

Oxford Magazine Vol.9, 1891.

Phelps MSS. Oriel College, Oxford.

Portus, G.V. 1983. *Happy Highways.* Melbourne.

Scott, E. 1936. *History of the University of Melbourne.* Melbourne.

Serle, P. 1949. *Dictionary of Australian Biography* Vol.II. Sydney.

Symonds, R. 1986. *Oxford and Empire.* London.

Turney, C. 1969. *Pioneers of Australian Education.* Sydney.

Whitington, F.T. 1887. *Augustus Short.* Adelaide.

Woolley, J. 1862. *Lectures Delivered in Australia.* London.

Figure 112. Sir Kenneth Wheare and kangaroo, dripstop on the Bodleian Library. Sir Kenneth Wheare was one of the Australians who stayed at Oxford though strongly maintaining his Australian identity. He was lecturer in Colonial History from 1935-1944, Gladstone Professor of Government from 1944 to 1957 and Rector of Exeter College from 1956 to 1972. He was Vice Chancellor of the University from 1964 to 1966. Thomas Photos.

8. Australians at Oxford

by John Legge

At first glance it may seem odd to include a chapter on Australians at Oxford in a volume prepared for Australia's bi-centennial year. Oxford's changing view of Australia: Yes. But Australian perceptions of Oxford were originally so much a part of the dependency syndrome that they may appear less than appropriate in a celebration of independent nationhood. Only at first glance, however. Independence, no matter how proudly proclaimed, had first to be achieved and changing attitudes to Britain – including changing attitudes to Britain's institutions of higher learning – are a part of whatever it is that is being celebrated in 1988.

Even as late as World War II the journey of Australian students to Oxford was part pilgrimage, in part the product of a judgment about the provinciality of Australian higher education and in part, more generally, a reflection of a particular order of power in the world at large. From the vantage point of 1988 it is not easy to recapture the very real sense of dependence on Britain of the first forty years of the Australian Commonwealth or to recall the slowness with which federated Australia, a self-governing Dominion within the Empire/Commonwealth, established genuine independence. There were classical issues at stake: questions of whether imperial unity could be reconciled with dominion self-government persisted in a variety of guises until almost the eve of World War II. Was the responsibility of dominion ministers to a dominion legislature consistent with the unity of Crown and Empire? Was there a half-way house between imperial federation and complete separation? Did a special British role in the defence of the Empire presuppose a special British responsiblity for the conduct of an imperial foreign policy? Might a Dominion's independent foreign policy involve Britain in conflicts not of her making?[1] Over time issues of this kind led to practical compromises in the light of such testing disagreements as were apparent at the Paris Peace Conference or in the Chanak crisis of 1922. A variety of formulations attempted to capture the realities of changing relationships: the idea of separate responsibility and common concern or the formula developed at the 1926 meeting of the Committee on Inter-Imperial Relations, which affirmed equality of status amongst members of the Commonwealth and described them as "in no way subordinate one to another in any aspect of their domestic or external affairs". But it was not until 1936 that Australia established her own Department of External Affairs. In 1939 Mr Menzies took the view that as Britain was at war Australia also was at war. And it was not until 1942 that Australia adopted the Statute of Westminster.

These preconceptions of a subordinate status were accurate enough for the time. It was a matter of simple fact that, for Australia, questions of peace and war were determined in Europe, that the threats to Australian security came from Mussolini's Italy and Hitler's Germany. Only with the changed power relationships of the postwar world would *de facto* independence from Britain really match the theoretical formulations of *de jure* independence developed by the constitutional lawyers (and be replaced, let it be admitted, by other forms of *de facto* dependence).

In the late 30s, then, Australian attitudes to Britain still had strong elements of attachment to a mother country: traditional loyalty, affection, a sense of kinship and the rest. The term "home" to refer to Britain was still current usage. And for many academically inclined young Australians the journey to Oxford was a part of that general outlook. As the possible crown to an Australian

---

[1] These questions received classical analysis at the hands of an Oxford Australian, W.K. Hancock in *Survey of British Commonwealth Affairs*, Vol I, *Problems of Nationality, 1918–1936.* (London, 1937).

university education it was compounded of a mixture of nostalgic yearning for an older tradition, a sense of remoteness from it and a view – no doubt a romantic view – of Oxford as the centre of traditional learning. It was Newman's idea of a university and Arnold's Oxford, steeped in sentiment and "whispering from her towers the last enchantments of the Middle Age", wrapped up together. The term "pilgrimage" is not inappropriate.

Cultural predispositions are apt to be resilient. The war shattered the framework within which these views were held; but they did not suddenly vanish as a result and, over a period, they adapted themselves to the new external and domestic circumstances. Within that changing context the pull of Oxford for Australian academia remained strong at least for a time, though it came gradually to fulfil different functions and to be perceived in a different light.

★   ★   ★

It would be interesting to trace in some detail, and through an examination of individual case histories, the nature of these changing functions and changing perceptions. What motivated Australian students who made that journey to Oxford after the war? What disciplines were most represented? Which colleges drew what sort of students? How many were graduate students and how many were taking a second bachelor's degree? What happened to them afterwards? Without such a close study what follows can at best be only an impressionistic picture.

In the postwar years, as before, some Australians, usually from more affluent backgrounds, went direct to Oxford from an Australian secondary education and had their first experience of university life at Magdalen (Malcolm Fraser) or Worcester (Rupert Murdoch) or Balliol (James Fairfax). More usually the Oxford experience followed tertiary education in Australia and for most was made possible only through the winning of a scholarship of one kind or another. The Rhodes was the most regular source, being tied specifically to

Oxford and, for Australians, being available to one student from each state each year. Other scholarships existed – Melbourne University's Aitcheson Travelling Scholarships, for example, or the Sir Arthur Sims Travelling Scholarhsip administered by the University of Melbourne but available to graduates from all Australian universities, or the University of Western Australia's Hackett Travelling Scholarships or the 1851 Exhibitions available to Australian postgraduate students. For the holders of these scholarships Oxford was merely one of the places that might be chosen. Some students went to London or to Cambridge. For a few years after 1948 the Australian National University, then in the process of formation, offered travelling scholarships specifically for graduate work overseas and some of these were taken up at Oxford. Those who did choose Oxford did so, sometimes, because of an individual scholar with whom they wanted to work and sometimes, no doubt, for what might be called sentimental reasons.

Was there any discernible preference shown by these students for one college over another? Did they tend to follow in each other's footsteps and to group themelves in particular colleges? Again, without a proper survey it is difficult to be sure who went where and for what reasons. In some disciplines students did appear to show a preference for a particular college, partly, no doubt, because of its reputation in that field, but also because of ties established earlier by their Australian teachers who might naturally advise them to apply to their old college and whose support could help them secure admission. Balliol, for example, attracted many historians. W.K. Hancock, Fred Alexander, Max Crawford, J.H. Reynolds, J.A. La Nauze and Manning Clark were all pre-war Balliol men and, in the postwar years, a stream of their students followed in their footsteps (Stretton, McBriar, Legge, Crowley, Burns, Williams, Mackay, Parnaby, Bastin, Phillips, Bolton, Raab, Groves and Davison were examples). Balliol's appeal for historians, especially for Melbourne historians, was a special case. Not all history students followed that route, of course (Shaw had been to Christ Church, Poynter and Knox went to Magdalen, Serle, Mackie and Inglis to Univ [2]) but the number who did is striking. In a similar way a number of philosophers – Benjamin, Baker, Bull, Dalrymple and others – chose University after George Paul had returned from his lectureship in Melbourne to take up a fellowship there. (Earlier, Cambridge had been the Mecca for Australian philosophers, again as a result of the links established by their teachers at home, but Paul, Strawson, Ryle and Austin changed that preference in the late 40s and early 50s.) Other students, however, distributed themselves across a range of houses without any noticeable pattern of discipline: Cole (Chemist) and Clarke (Biologist) to St John's, Durack (Law) to Lincoln, Deb Newton (English) and Margaret Kerr (History) to LMH, Leonie Gibson (English) to St Hugh's, Bob Hawke (PPE) to Univ, Kit McMahon (PPE) to Magdalen, Zelman Cowen (Law) to New College and Oriel, Alison Hale (History) to St Hilda's, Crisp (PPE) and Scott (English) to Balliol, Roderick Carnegie (PPE) to New College. One could extend the list indefinitely.

During the postwar years a change could be seen in the patterns of study of Australian students. Before the war the normal course for humanities and social science students, even if they already possessed a first class degree from an Australian university, was to read PPE or History or English, and science graduates, too, tended to proceed to a first degree once again. In the postwar years the same pattern continued for some historians, economists, philosophers and political scientists. Quite a few philosophers and some historians were attracted by the new B.Phil. when it was introduced in 1947. As a degree by examination rather than by thesis, it seemed to offer the traditional method of regular contact between individual student and tutor, rather than the less structured supervision of the research

degree. But postwar natural scientists almost universally engaged in research for the D.Phil., and increasingly students in the humanities and social sciences followed that example. This was a reflection of the importance of a research training for potential academics and it accompanied the development of graduate schools in Australian universities. The Ph.D. as a meal ticket was on the way and Australians in Oxford adjusted accordingly.

The choice – Schools or D.Phil. – had obvious consequences for the nature of the Oxford experience. Oxford, after all, was by tradition geared to the training of undergraduates, fitting them, whether by Firsts or Seconds or sporting Fourths, for entry to public life, the professions, the senior ranks of the home civil service or for the task of ruling the Empire. The College system and the relationship of undergraduates to individual teachers, the weekly essay, the relations with other undergraduates aided by the staircase organization, dining requirements and the buttery, were all part of that. It was a system of comparatively small communities living in civilized relationships and forming bonds that would be maintained in the future. Australians reading for Schools were absorbed with varying degrees of completeness into that way of life. They might occasionally be irritated by Oxford's academic rituals, and remain determinedly unimpressed by elegant pretension and, in brash and self-confident manner, try to cut through the nonsense. They were likely to mock the local vocabulary ("What am I reading? Well, an Agatha Christie just at the moment.") And there were social problems too. Some may have felt uncomfortable at first in establishing appropriate relations with their scouts, and they were likely to maintain an amused scepticism about the customs of the young gentlemen about them. Were they in some respects more comfortable with the scholarship students, or with Scots, north countrymen, Americans, Canadians and Indians, than with the products of the English upper middle classes? Or did they feel themselves to be outside the class system and therfore able

[2] Inglis' choice of college, he says, was made solely on the basis of the flexibility of its residence requirements for married students!

91

more easily to move freely across class boundaries? Many did fall into the latter category and used an Australian informality of manner to sustain relaxed and easy friendships with a wide range of people. There were those, of course, who embraced the new life style with enthusiasm, changing their accents in the process and modelling themselves on the world of *Brideshead Revisted*. The equal and opposite reaction was to become more ocker than ever, seeking acceptance by outraging the natives. However in one way or another most Australians managed to achieve a satisfactory accommodation. And the system was tolerant enough and flexible enough to make them an integral part of itself.

It was not so, at least in the early postwar years, for the research student in the humanities and social sciences. Oxford was not, at that time, really organized for graduate supervision and the life of the advanced student was likely to be a lonely one unless deliberate action was taken to prevent it. As often as not research students found themselves assigned to a supervisor in another college. Their meetings with supervisors were fairly casual and infrequent. There were some method seminars, but well trained students from Australian universities sometimes found these to be less sophisticated than those they had attended in the course of their Australian Honours degrees. There were other seminars, learned of through the lecture schedule, to which they could attach themselves if they chose. But these things had to be arranged deliberately. They did not simply happen. Some handled the problem by disappearing into the Bodleian or the basement of the Rhodes House Library for the duration. Others took conscious action to establish for themselves a network of contacts among other graduate students and dons. Others again, by means of living in college, worked at developing undergraduate contacts and living as far as possible an undergraduate life while working as graduate students. That was not as easy as it sounds. Australians taking a second bachelor's degree,

even though older than their English fellows, were drawn by common subject matter and common reading and essay requirements into a close and continuing relationship with them, argued with them over coffee in the Junior Common Room, drank with them in the Turf or the Lamb and Flag, the Eagle and Child or the King's Arms, and entered into their pattern of sporting and social activities. A graduate student lacked those regular and natural points of contact and did, indeed, have to work at developing undergraduate friendships and moving in undergraduate circles. For the married graduate student – and a greater proportion of Australians in postwar Oxford were already married on arrival than had been the case in the past – the task was more difficult. They necessarily lived outside College for the whole of their Oxford period and lacked the natural points of entry.

This was gradually to change. The introduction of the B.Phil. has already been mentioned as one way of responding to the needs of students who had already graduated elsewhere; and during the 50s Oxford moved specifically to adapt to the special requirements of its growing number of research students. The extended provision of formal graduate seminars in a variety of fields provided the regular framework of study and interaction that had been lacking before. As one example, the Imperial History seminar developed by Gallagher as Beit Professor and continued by Robinson, his successor in the Chair, transformed the working relationships of graduate students in that field. The mere fact of increasing numbers in itself meant the existence of a community with its own corporate sense. The expanding role of Nuffield contributed to the changed atmosphere. In the 40s and early 50s many Australians enjoyed Nuffield affiliation while belonging to another college, and in due course Nuffield admitted its own graduate students and provided a collegiate setting for them. With these developments it was no longer necessary for graduate students to attempt to

Figure 113. The Radcliffe Camera and the spire of St. Mary's. (Chris Andrews)

merge themselves into the undergraduate body, though college residence still made that possible for some. Whether living in college or in digs, whether at Nuffield or elsewhere, the research student could belong satisfactorily to a sizeable and congenial research student community.

At the end of their Oxford experience the overwhelming majority of Oxford Australians returned more or less immediately to Australia. Whether this was by choice or necessity, a matter of being glad to get home or of going where career opportunities were likely to be found, cannot be determined and it is true that some of them did stay permanently in the United Kingdom and can be found in positions ranging from College Fellow to Deputy Governor of the Bank of England. But perhaps it may be assumed that, however seductive the appeal of the metropolis, the natural move was back to an Australian career. It would be interesting to carry out a detailed survey of their various destinations, but the ranks include one Governor General, two Prime Ministers, some businessmen, members of parliament, civil servants (including one former head of Treasury) and a small army of academics. The pursuit of a higher degree by many suggested the hope of an academic career and this was indeed the goal of a great number of Oxford's Australians in the postwar period. Many ended up in Chairs or other senior positions in a wide range of disciplines. There were some who moved to and fro between England and Australia. Max Hartwell went from Oxford to the foundation Chair of Humanities in the new New South Wales University of Technology (later to become the University of New South Wales) but then returned to a Fellowship at Nuffield. Bob O'Neill went from BNC to the Department of International Relations at the Australian National University and then returned to head the International Institute of Strategic Studies in London, and, subsequently, to become Chichele Professor of the History of War. Zelman Cowen took up an Oriel Fellowship immediately after his Oxford graduation, but he then moved to a Melbourne Chair of Law,

to two vice-chancellorships in succession and to the Governor Generalship, before returning ultimately to Oxford as Provost of Oriel. These, however, were exceptions. For the most part the benefits of study in Oxford were to be reinvested in one way or another permanently at home.

★   ★   ★

Since the early postwar years, though Oxford has caught up with other places in meeting the needs of its graduate students and has continued to attract a substantial undergraduate contingent from Australia, it is probable that ties between Oxford and Australian academia have weakened. Rhodes scholars continue. The Rhodes terms of reference have broadened to include women as have those of the formerly male colleges. And holders of other travelling scholarships still choose Oxford. Awards under the Commonwealth Scholarships and Fellowships Plan enabled students from one Commonwealth country to study in another and this could apply to Australians wishing to study in the United Kingdom. For social scientists Nuffield provides a powerful attraction. But the idea of Oxford as one of the major places on which Australian students would be likely to set their sights has had to compete with the pull of other places and other goals.

This has been due in part to educational developments taking place within Australia itself. The creation of the Australian National University as a purely research institution opened new opportunities for graduate work within its four research schools, Physical Sciences, Medical Research, Social Sciences and Pacific Studies. (In 1961, after amalgamation with the Canberra University College, the research schools, with three additional members, became the Institute of Advanced Studies within the ANU.) There followed the exciting transformation of the whole University scene as a result of the Murray Committee Report of 1958. The rapid expansion in the number of universities, from 9 in the mid-50s to 19 today, the consequent opportunity for experiment and innovation, the accompanying

Figure 114. The curve of the High. Woodmansterne/Malcolm Osman.

development of strong graduate schools in the humanities and social sciences as well as in the natural sciences and the creation of generous post-graduate scholarship schemes (generous at least by the standards of the 40s and 50s) have combined simultaneously to increase dramatically the size of the annual post-graduate cohort and to keep most of its members within Australia, either by encouraging them to continue with advanced work within their original departments or to go elsewhere in Australia for master's or doctoral work.

Australian graduates returning from Oxford had a part to play in these developments, providing many of the senior appointments in the new universities where they saw themselves as simultaneously preserving traditional academic values and pioneering new methods. Their success in the first of these goals may be reflected, perhaps, in a recent criticism by a federal Industry minister who should have known better, that

Australian universities had inherited a British academic tradition of "splendid isolation", spending a disproportionate amount of activity on basic research. Leaving aside the question-begging aspects of that accusation – what after all is the correct proportion? – and leaving aside also the unpredictable nature of the links between basic research and the utilitarian applications that might flow from it later, there has in fact been plenty of concern for policy issues on the part of Australian social scientists and plenty of mission-oriented research in the natural sciences, and, in gerneral, the reverse of splended isolation.

Parallel with the growth of post-graduate opportunities within Australian universities was the perception of America as the home of some of the world's major centres of learning. Whereas an earlier generation of Australian students had, without much question, regarded study in England as the goal to be pursued, and had limited their choices pretty much to Oxford, Cambridge

95

and London, a later generation had a sense of much wider choice. And whereas the earlier choices had perhaps tended to be essentially choices of place as such, rather than of teachers and subjects, the later choices were probably made more in terms of where a chosen field or subject could best be studied. The earlier generation went to Oxford or Cambridge or London because it was Oxford or Cambridge or London, and course of study or topics of research followed that choice. The new generation thought in terms of specialized interests which would take them perhaps to Oxford or perhaps to Berkeley or Yale or Cornell.

All of this took place, of course, in a changed international context in which Australia, no longer protected by the might of British sea power, attempted to shape her own independent approach to the world, to accommodate herself to the turbulence of her immediate region, and to look for long term protection to her great and powerful ally across the Pacific. Curtin's appeal to the United States in 1941 had indeed constituted a fundamental wrench of perspective. No longer could Britain be viewed as the centre of Australia's universe. And there were other changes which reinforced that. Immigration patterns after World War II have altered the complexion of Australian society and diluted the notion of Australians as "transplanted British". [3] By the 60s Japan had replaced Britain as Australia's principal trading partner. Changes in the speed and accessibility of transport have ended the earlier remoteness and made it no longer an exceptional thing for Australians to make the journey to Europe. Gone is the experience of encountering the outside world for the first time in Colombo, Aden and Port Said. What was once a four week journey is now an overnight hop and the grand tour or a working holiday is not an impossible dream. And on the grand tour Oxford is one place amongst others to be seen.

These changes of general perspective have altered the way in which Oxford is viewed from an Australian university. Nevertheless their effect must not be exaggerated. Oxford may now be regarded as one centre of learning amongst many others, it may now have to compete with a wider world of scholarship, Australian and American, for Australian scholars. Its attractions are no longer underpinned as effectively as they once were by sentiment or by notions of imperial kinship. It retains, nevertheless its own excellence, its own distinctive methods and, of course, its own beauty. Even the nostalgia of Arnold's romantic picture can have its place and Australians will continue to enjoy the purely physical pleasure of the city. The enjoyment of walking up the High from Magdalen Bridge and watching the curve of the street unwind must be one of the great experiences of urban townscape. Or the walk down Catte Street in which, as Thomas Sharp pointed out, the cube of the Bodleian, the cylinder and dome of the Radcliffe Camera and the cone of St Mary's spire deploy themselves suddenly and simultaneously. [4] One could extend the catalogue endlessly: the walk through Port Meadow to Godstow, the walk along Mesopotamia in the the spring, the New College cloister.

For a complex of reasons, then, Oxford will continue to be chosen by some Australians. Students in particular fields will go there because that is where those fields are best studied or because of the reputation of individual scholars. It will be chosen by others because of the type of undergraduate experience it can offer. And some, no doubt, will recognize a continuing tradition which may still seem relevant to the intellectual needs even of a late 20th century Australian.

---

[3] W.K. Hancock's term. *Australia* (1930).

[4] Thomas Sharp, *Oxford Replanned* (1948).